Literacies, Power and Identities in Figured Worlds in Malawi

Adult Learning, Literacy and Social Change

SERIES EDITORS:

Anna Robinson-Pant (University of East Anglia, UK)
Alan Rogers (University of East Anglia, UK and University of Nottingham, UK)

This series explores the complex relationship between adult learning and social change. Instead of the common focus on adult literacy as kick-starting development, the series considers how adult learning and literacy can also emerge from processes of social change. Each volume introduces new theoretical and methodological lenses to investigate insights into adult learning and literacy based on original empirical research by the authors. Recognising that Governments from the Global North as well as the Global South have recently signed up to the Sustainable Development Goals, this series brings together research conducted in a wide range of countries, including Malawi, Nepal, China, the Philippines and the UK.

ADVISORY BOARD:

Dennis Banda (University of Zambia, Zambia)
Lesley Bartlett (University of Wisconsin, USA)
Maria Lucia Castanheira (Federal University of Minas Gerais, Brazil)
Mostafa Hasrati (Seneca College, Canada)
Li Jiacheng (East China Normal University, China)
Judy Kalman (CINVESTAV, Mexico)
Simon McGrath (University of Nottingham, UK)
Tonic Maruatona (University of Botswana, Botswana)
Tony Mays (Commonwealth of Learning)
Hendrik Nordvall (Mimer, The Swedish Network for Research on Popular Education, Sweden)
Mastin Prinsloo (University of Cape Town, South Africa)
Anita Rampal (University of Delhi, India)
Bonnie Slade (University of Glasgow, UK)

Also available in the series:

Migrant Workers' Education in China: Changing Discourses and Practices,
by Fusheng Jia
Literacies, Power and Identities in Figured Worlds in Malawi,
by Ahmmardouh Mjaya

Forthcoming in the series:

Adult Learning and Social Change in the UK: National and Local Perspectives,
edited by Jules Robbins and Alan Rogers

Literacies, Power and Identities in Figured Worlds in Malawi

Ahmmardouh Mjaya

BLOOMSBURY ACADEMIC
LONDON • NEW YORK • OXFORD • NEW DELHI • SYDNEY

BLOOMSBURY ACADEMIC
Bloomsbury Publishing Plc
50 Bedford Square, London, WC1B 3DP, UK
1385 Broadway, New York, NY 10018, USA
29 Earlsfort Terrace, Dublin 2, Ireland

BLOOMSBURY, BLOOMSBURY ACADEMIC and the Diana logo are
trademarks of Bloomsbury Publishing Plc

First published in Great Britain 2022
This paperback edition published 2023

Copyright © Ahmmardouh Mjaya, 2022

Ahmmardouh Mjaya has asserted his right under the Copyright,
Designs and Patents Act, 1988, to be identified as Author of this work.

For legal purposes the Acknowledgements on p. xiv constitute
an extension of this copyright page.

Cover design: Charlotte James

All rights reserved. No part of this publication may be reproduced or transmitted
in any form or by any means, electronic or mechanical, including photocopying,
recording, or any information storage or retrieval system, without prior
permission in writing from the publishers.

Bloomsbury Publishing Plc does not have any control over, or responsibility for,
any third-party websites referred to or in this book. All internet addresses given in this
book were correct at the time of going to press. The author and publisher regret any
inconvenience caused if addresses have changed or sites have ceased to exist,
but can accept no responsibility for any such changes.

A catalogue record for this book is available from the British Library.

A catalog record for this book is available from the Library of Congress.

ISBN: HB: 978-1-3501-4481-1
       PB: 978-1-3502-9617-6
       ePDF: 978-1-3501-4483-5
       eBook: 978-1-3501-4484-2

Series: Adult Learning, Literacy and Social Change

Typeset by Integra Software Services Pvt. Ltd.

To find out more about our authors and books visit www.bloomsbury.com
and sign up for our newsletters.

Contents

List of Figures	vi
Preface	vii
Series Foreword	ix
Literacies, Power and Identities in Figured Worlds in Malawi	xii
Acknowledgements	xiv
Abbreviations	xv
1 'Schools of Day Break': A Research Context	1
2 Power and Identity: Exploring Theoretical Perspectives	13
3 'Being there': Dilemmas and Opportunities	29
4 Literacy Practices in Community Members' Lived Worlds	53
5 Identities and Power in Reading and Writing Spaces	71
6 The Adult Literacy Class: A Site of Power Struggle	91
7 'Mbecete M'ciyawo': Language Use in Literacy Classrooms	109
8 Literacy, Power and Identity in Figured Worlds	125
References	147
Index	159

Figures

1	Chichewa Lesson	32
2	Cluster of Houses for the Weca Family	37
3	Sawabu Literacy Class	40
4	Malekano Trading Centre	42
5	Wooden Bridge to Cipago across Kasupe River	43
6	Video Showroom at Malekano	44
7	Tupoce Clinic	45
8	Ration Card	55
9	An Agricultural Leaflet	57
10	Spacing in a Maize Garden	58
11	Registration Slip	60
12	The Malawi Social Cash Transfer Programme Leaflet (Outer pages)	61
13	The Malawi Social Cash Transfer Programme Leaflet (Inner pages)	62
14	Beneficiary Money Card (Inner pages)	63
15	Ms Msosa's Book	75
16	Road Sign	122
17	Blue Chlorine Dispenser	133

Preface

From Linguistics to Literacy: A Shift that Never was

Looking back and reflecting on my journey into literacy research, I am fascinated by not only the multiple and diverse identities I have had but also the shifts and turns that characterized the research processes whose data is used in this book.

My journey into literacy studies began when I joined the Centre for Language Studies (CLS) at Chancellor College in the University of Malawi as a Ciyawo[1] Language Specialist in 2004. As a language specialist, my major role is to conduct research in language and language-related issues. But owing to shortages of staff in the Department of African Languages and Linguistics, I was also expected to help in lecturing some linguistics courses in the Department. For to perform these there was need to upgrade my academic qualifications. I therefore, enrolled for a part-time Master's Degree in Applied Linguistics at the same college. As I studied for this degree, I was also taking part in developing a national language in education policy for the country which the Ministry of Education asked CLS to formulate.

Most of the arguments we raised during our discussions regarding language of instruction in lower primary revolved around a speedy acquisition of initial literacy and meaningful understanding of lessons. At that time, mother tongue instruction was deemed to be the best way forward. These discussions, coupled with the exposure I had to literature on adult literacy during my course work, propelled me to do a dissertation on the choice and use of minority languages in adult literacy programmes, that is, 'language that is not the dominant language of a territorial unit such as a state, because the speakers of the language have less power … and [which] is generally spoken by a smaller number of people' (Skutnabb-Kangas & McCarty, 2006: 7) especially Ciyawo, in adult literacy. This dissertation marked the beginning of not only my interest in literacy research but also my new identity as a literacy researcher, such that when the Centre for Advanced Studies of African Societies (CASAS) asked my faculty to carry

---

[1] I am Yawo by tribe and the language of the Yawo is called Ciyawo.

out a pilot adult literacy support initiative, I was nominated to oversee its implementation (for more details about CASAS, see http://www.casas.co.za/).

The pilot initiative involved supplying to the literacy learners some supplementary readers written in local languages with a view to helping them to consolidate their new literacies. What struck me most when I assessed the initiative was that the adult literacy learners wanted materials that covered topics which were apparently not included in their official primers. This gave me the impression that there was a certain degree of disjuncture between what the programme offered and what the learners desired to learn.

Meanwhile, when in 2010, the Malawi Government gave me an opportunity to study for another Master's degree, I decided to do a full-time course in adult literacy at the University of East Anglia (UEA). Somehow, my decision to venture into literacy appeared to raise some questions from some of my superiors. They queried the links between literacy and my jobs as a language specialist and lecturer in linguistics. At that time, I struggled to craft a response. Yet, to attest the value of local languages, my centre was using literacy as a benchmark, albeit in a narrow sense. Arguments were being made that 'initial literacy in one's most familiar language aids the acquisition of literacy in a second or foreign language' (Ministry of Education, 2007: 7).

As I studied for my degree, I was firmly exposed to the New Literacy Studies (NLS) as well as to contemporary literacy orientations and literacy research paradigms such as ethnography. I came to understand that literacy and language are strongly intertwined. I realized how futile and partial it is for us to talk about literacy without paying attention to language.

As I wrote my dissertation for my second MA degree through the lens of literacy as a social practice, I got a sense that there were many aspects of literacy in general, and Malawi's National Adult Literacy Programme (NALP) in particular, that I needed to understand further. Therefore, when a chance arose for me to study for a PhD at UEA, I decided to carry on exploring literacy practices within the context of the NALP in Malawi. Unlike my MA whose focus was on understanding literacy policy discourses, my PhD thesis dwelt on literacy, power and identities in literacy practices in the NALP.

The biggest lesson I learned from these studies is that indeed, literacy and language are intertwined. The shift that was feared never took place. I am still who I was, a linguist, teaching among others, literacy and language, in the Department of African Languages and Linguistics at Chancellor College, University of Malawi.

Series Foreword

Adult Learning, Literacy and Social Change

This series explores the complex relationship between adult learning, literacy and social change through empirical research conducted within and beyond educational programmes in a wide range of countries in the Global North and South. Since the launch of the 2030 Sustainable Development Goals, there has been growing interest in how adult literacy – sometimes referred to as 'the invisible glue' (LWG 2007) – connects the seventeen goals. Much research has focused on how to measure literacy progress quantitatively (through literacy rates) against such development indicators and assumed that most literacy learning takes place formally within institutions or educational programmes. Rather than taking this instrumental approach, this series investigates the 'why' and 'how' of the assumed relationship between adult learning, literacy and social change.

The UNESCO Chair in Adult Literacy and Learning for Social Transformation (based at University of East Anglia, UK) has strongly shaped the approach and stance of this series. Aiming to develop understanding about how adult literacy and learning – particularly for women and young adults – can help address inequalities in the poorest communities of the world, the UNESCO Chair brings together university departments specializing in adult literacy and community learning in the UK, Ethiopia, Nepal, Malawi, Egypt and the Philippines. Several of the books in this series emerged from in-depth qualitative research studies conducted by researchers within this international partnership.

Providing a much-needed critical perspective on adult literacy and development, the series challenges the usual starting point of international and national policy discourse and research in this field. First, the shift to consider social change rather than development offers a broader, holistic lens, since 'development' implies a limited perspective on social change as predetermined, planned, staged and often with an envisaged endpoint (Castles, 2001). Conceptual debate on 'social transformation' (defined as 'big' social change by Haas *et al*, 2020) informs this analysis – particularly the notion that 'social transformations are deeply political in nature, an insight which dominant, "technocratic" development theories and ideologies ignore and actively try to conceal' (ibid: 7). This alternative lens provides a way to step outside development frameworks that focus only on literacy and development outcomes, in order to recentre attention onto people's lived experiences of social change.

Secondly, this series is grounded on an 'ideological' rather than an 'autonomous' model of literacy (Street, 1984). In contrast to much international development policy and research which has drawn on an understanding of literacy as decontextualized skills learned in a classroom, the series takes a 'situated' approach (Barton, Hamilton and Ivanic, 2000) to investigate literacy and adult learning in everyday life. Researching informal and nonformal learning – both within and beyond educational institutions and development programmes – the authors offer original insights into how adults are engaging with an ever-increasing diversity of literacies, languages, cultural values and technologies. Resisting the common tendency to conflate literacy, learning and education, they explore the complex relationships around power, knowledge and identities that are shaping people's lives and social change.

Thirdly, this series accepts the now widely held view of adult learning as comprising formal, non-formal and informal elements (UNESCO, 2009: 27); not necessarily as discrete activities but often inextricably mixed in a lifelong and lifewide process of interaction between social members. Learning can no longer be seen as the sole prerogative of educational institutions in time-limited activities; it takes multiple forms and occurs in multiple locations throughout life. The volumes in this series will explore how such adult learning is inspired by and at the same time contributes to social change.

As the world now grapples with the devastating effects of the global Covid-19 pandemic, climate change, conflict, migration and widening inequalities, the focus of this series is particularly relevant. More than ever before, social change is seen as unpredictable, and new educational challenges are emerging. The authors in this series do not set out to advocate solutions for policy makers or educational providers. However, these in-depth research accounts share rich first-hand experiences, observations, analysis and voices that are often unheard, thereby introducing new ways to understand adult learning, literacy and social change.

Anna Robinson-Pant
Alan Rogers

References

Barton, D., Hamilton, M. and R. Ivanic (2000) *Situated Literacies: Reading and Writing in Context,* London: Routledge

Castles, S. (2001) Studying Social Transformation, *International Political Science Review,* Vol. 22, No. 1, pp 13–32

Haas, H., Fransen, S., Natter, K., Schewel, K., and Vezzoli, S. (2020) *Social Transformation,* International Migration Institute Working Papers, Paper 166, July 2020, Oxford: IMI

Street, B.V. (1984) *Literacy in Theory and Practice,* Cambridge: Cambridge University Press

University of East Anglia UNESCO Chair: https://www.uea.ac.uk/groups-and-centres/unesco-chair-programme

UK Literacy Working Group (2007) Literacy and international development: the next steps, LWG Position Paper, available at: http://balid.org.uk/pdfs/LWG%20Position%20Paper%20Final%20June07%20CD%20final.doc

UNESCO. (2009) *Global Report on Adult Learning and Education,* Hamburg: UIL

Literacies, Power and Identities in Figured Worlds in Malawi

This is the first volume to appear in the series on Adult Learning, Literacy and Social Change. The series aims to explore – through qualitative research – some of the complexities between these three concepts.

Dr Ahmmadouh Mjaya of Chancellor College, Malawi, has explored literacy practices in a small village in Malawi through in-depth ethnographic research. He situates the experiences of women attending an adult literacy class in the broader context of their community, including the various development and relief programmes being implemented there. By taking the concept of 'figured worlds' (Holland *et al*, 1998), he investigates power relationships and identities in activities where people had to engage with reading and writing in their everyday lives – such as the ration cards for relief food or the registration slip for the Malawi Social Cash Transfer Programme – as well as within an adult literacy programme. This is not a story of a development initiative with predetermined goals; rather it is an account of how these women view literacy and how they use the artefacts of literacy (conceptualized in terms of a 'figured world') which they see as imbued with significance in different contexts within their everyday lives. Ahmmardouh Mjaya's contribution is to illuminate how the literacy programme/class was just one 'figured world' where people in this village learned and used written texts.

In this way, this volume contributes to the goals of the series. It speaks to and against the dominant discourse on adult literacy and development through illustrating that literacy is wider than learning to read and write in a classroom. It views social change with a wider lens than 'development'. The author sees adult learning and literacy as taking place not just in a formal classroom but in nonformal activities and in informal (lifelong and lifewide) learning in the everyday hustle and bustle of community life; and it sees literacy as a set of practices which change according to different contexts – in other words, as 'situated literacy practices'.

Dr Mjaya spent ten months living within this community; as the book title indicates, he sought to explore identities – not just those of the women literacy learners and their teachers, but also his own identities as an ethnographic researcher, university lecturer and neighbour. And these identities are expressed through various voices – those of the women themselves, of the managers of the literacy learning programme and of course his own voice as researcher and colleague. And through it all, he is conscious of power – how all relationships ultimately express something of the power within.

Importantly, this study demonstrates the great value of such situated ethnographic approaches to researching adult literacy learning – supported by the now established body of literature within the so-called 'new' literacy studies. By showing that one adult literacy class in a Malawian village had such a range of experiences as described in this book, the author is raising questions about adult learning, literacy and social change which may be asked of all adult literacy classes – in the Global North and Global South.

This book launches a series which sets out to provide a much-needed critical perspective on adult literacy and development, offering new ways to understand adult literacy, learning and social change. All over the world, people are embracing social change and there is a pressing need for effective forms of adult learning and literacy to direct such changes towards greater inclusiveness, less social inequalities and wider social justice. This book is not just of relevance for those working in Sub-Saharan Africa, but for all who are interested in adult learning, literacy and social change.

Anna Robinson-Pant
Alan Rogers

Acknowledgements

As the author of this book, I sincerely thank the editors for their encouragement, guidance and support during the time when I was experiencing various difficulties and the prospects of finalizing this book appeared to be waning. I am also grateful to Prof. Pascal Kishindo and late Prof. Paul Kishindo for supporting and making me feel confident in my decision to venture into literacy study.

I also wish to express my heartfelt gratitude to NALP officers at Zomba district office, the instructors, the supervisor, the literacy learners at Sawabu literacy centre and village headperson Sawabu for giving me permission to conduct my study in Sawabu village in general and Sawabu literacy centre in particular. Special thanks go to all community members in Sawabu village for sharing and allowing me to use their lived experiences in my work wholeheartedly.

Abbreviations

CSSC	Community Social Support Committee
FAO	Food and Agriculture Organisation
FISP	Farm Input Subsidy Programme
FGD	Focus Group Discussion
ICEIDA	Icelandic International Development Agency
MA	Master of Arts
MCP	Malawi Congress Party
MP	Member of Parliament
NALP	National Adult Literacy Programme
NCLAE	National Centre for Literacy and Adult Education
NGO	Non-Governmental Organisation
NLS	New Literacy Studies
OSISA	Open Society Initiative for Southern Africa
PAP	Poverty Alleviation Programme
PhD	Doctor of Philosophy
PRRO	Protracted Relief and Recovery Operation
REFLECT	Regenerated Freirean Literacy through Empowering Community Techniques
STAR	Societies Tackling Aids through Rights
UEA	University of East Anglia
UNDP	United Nations Development Programme
UNESCO	United Nations Education, Scientific and Cultural Organisation
WCEFA	World Conference on Education For All
WFP	World Food Programme

1

'Schools of Day Break': A Research Context

I do not understand why some women do not want to attend literacy lessons. It is shameful that some of them print using their thumbs to receive fertilizer coupons. Old women who are attending the literacy classes surprised clerks last year when they asked for pens to sign their names to receive the coupons. I am happy that I am attending these classes because before doing so I did not know anything.

(Ms Maulidi; Field notes: 22 September 2015)

This extract captures the views expressed by many community members I interacted with during my fieldwork and it reveals that the community members had diverse expectations from their literacy class some of which diverged from the official perspectives of the literacy programme, thereby raising the question as to who had the power to decide what counts as literacy. At the same time some community members appeared to use their literacy learning as a means to redefine their literacy identity. As an attendee of *Sukulu ya Kwacha* (school of daybreak i.e. literacy class), Ms Maulidi appeared to re-examine her self-image. She appreciated her perceived transformation from someone who did not know anything (ignorant) to the one who knew something (the educated/enlightened; more discussions on this later in this chapter).

The focus of my initial PhD research proposal was directed towards understanding adult literacy policy in Malawi. What I saw as a problem at that time was the apparent lack of efforts in understanding how the 'graduates' from the National Adult Literacy Programme (NALP) use their newly acquired literacy. My overall aim was to establish how the newly acquired competences helped to improve the lives of the learners. As I searched for more literature to gain a better understanding of my topic, I encountered new questions concerning both the NALP in Malawi and the social theory of literacy as well.

As far as the NALP was concerned, I noted that literacy studies based on the social theory of literacy were hardly conducted in Malawi. At the same time, my review of the theoretical literature brought to the fore some critiques which suggested that, although issues of power and identity in literacy practices are highlighted and discussed in New Literacy Studies (NLS), they are often underemphasized in research accounts because, among other things, the social theory of literacy itself appears not to have developed clear and detailed analytical tools (see Chapter 2). I, therefore, decided to change my research focus although the context and the theory underpinning the study remained the same buttressed by Holland, Lachicotte Jr., Skinner and Cain's (1998) theory of self and identity especially the notion of figured world. My aim was to explore how the concept of figured world can help us investigate and understand better the social and situated nature of literacy. Specifically, the study sought to address the following questions:

- How can community members' literacy practices be explored using the concept of figured world?
- To what extent can the concept of figured world help us in understanding community members' literacy meanings and discourses?
- How do literacy practices shape power relations among community members; how can such relations be unpacked through the concept of figured world?
- At local level, what implications for policy and practice can be drawn from literacy studies based on the concept of figured world?

Having conducted some studies on the NALP in Malawi, I decided to do this research in Zomba, Malawi, because of two main reasons. First, I wanted to carry on and deepen my understanding of the NALP in the country. Second, I had already established a working relationship with some NALP gatekeepers in Zomba which meant that it would be easier for me to gain access.

As a novice ethnographer, deciding between breadth and depth was one of the key issues I struggled to deal with. Initially, I chose the former by planning to have multiple research sites but later realized that within the limited time I had, I would learn very little and therefore decided to have one site, namely Sawabu village (more details about the research site are given in Chapter 3).

Malawi: Just at a glance

Malawi is a small landlocked country situated in the southern part of Africa. The country shares borders with Tanzania to the north, Zambia to the west and Mozambique to the east and south. It has twenty-eight administrative districts spread across its southern, central and northern regions. The country has four cities namely Mzuzu in the north, Lilongwe, (the capital city) in the centre and Blantyre and Zomba in the south.

The World Bank classifies Malawi as one of the poorest in the world. With a population of about 18 million and a population density of 186 persons per square kilometre (National Statistical Office, 2019), the country's economy depends on agriculture which employs about 80 per cent of the population. Eighty-four per cent of the Malawians live in the rural areas and they contribute about 70 per cent of the agricultural produce.

Realizing the assumed significance of literacy in fostering development, including in the efforts to increase agricultural productivity (see Government of Malawi, 2012), the Malawi government has been offering lessons to individuals assumed to be non-literate from as early as 1947. This has been the case because although the literacy rates have been improving in terms of percentages (currently at 69 per cent), the number of individuals presumed to be non-literate has been growing steadily (4,700,000 in 2018; see National Statistical Office, 2019). The situation is exacerbated by high rates of school dropouts, with many young people leaving school before acquiring basic literacy skills (see Government of Malawi, 2011). In fact, results from the Southern and East African Consortium for Monitoring Education Quality (SACMEQ) learning assessment survey show that 63.6 per cent of Malawian grade six pupils were not able to read for meaning (Milner, Mulera, Chimuzu Banda, Mutale and Chimombo, 2011).

Linguistically, Malawi is a multilingual nation with about sixteen languages spoken in various parts of the country. However, as a former British colony, English is the official language alongside a local language, Chichewa. What this means is that Chichewa and English are the only languages which are formally tolerated in official contexts.

Literacy research in Malawi

In Malawi, research in literacy in general and in adult literacy in particular has been minimal such that the bulk of literature on this subject come from evaluation reports focusing more on assessing the effectiveness and efficiency of the programmes in line with the government's development objectives (see Mpheluka, 1983; Kuthemba Mwale, 1990; Center for Social Research, 2000; Phiri & Safaraoh 2003; Benediktsson & Kamtengeni, 2004; Dulani & Chinsinga, 2006; Jeke, 2006; OSISA, 2007).

One of the major assumptions underlying these studies has been that the rural populations have some deficits which could seemingly be fixed through the attainment of a particular type of literacy. Thus, consistent with what Street (1993) calls the autonomous model of literacy, the researchers have often appeared to promote the understanding which perceives literacy as a single entity which can be learned in one context and be applied anywhere it is needed, and that its benefits stem from within it. They assume that a successful adult literacy programme is the one that attracts many adult literacy learners who eventually succeed in mastering the government's privileged literacy skills. But some critics argue that success should not be determined by just focusing on the competences gained but also on whether such skills are used in daily activities (Rogers, Kachiwanda & McKay, 2003).

Generally, the impact of these studies has been negligible, especially when we consider the fact that almost all of them raise the same key challenges such as lack of training for instructors, high withdrawal rates, low participation of men, low funding, inefficient monitoring, and evaluation of literacy classes and, in the end, make similar recommendations. Suffice to say that the Malawi government appears to have realized the importance of systematic literacy studies beyond evaluating the NALP. Thus, it calls for 'the need to expand the research base so that policies on literacy and adult education can be based on empirical research' (Ministry of Gender, Child Welfare and Community Services, 2004: iv). In line with this call, recently there have been some literacy studies which have focused on some critical aspects of literacy such as language use, literacy discourses and motivations of adults for taking part in literacy lessons (see Kamtengeni, 1999; Kachiwanda, 2009; Mjaya, 2010 & 2011).

Elsewhere, since the 1980s, the understanding of literacy has evolved from perceiving it as just a set of stand-alone skills to viewing it as a social practice (see Chapter 2). In the same vein, literacy studies have shifted from just assessing how best to help non-literate individuals to acquire literacy towards focusing more on the voice and literacy lived experiences of the literacy learners (see Street, 1984; Prinsloo & Breier, 1996; Barton & Hamilton 1998; Robinson-Pant, 2001a; Papen, 2002; Millican, 2004; Kalman, 2005a; Gebre, Rogers, Street, & Openjuru, 2009; Nabi, Rogers, & Street, 2009; Openjuru, Baker, Rogers, & Street, 2016).

This book is based on a ten-month in-depth ethnographic study of literacy practices in a small village in Malawi. The focus of the study was on literacy learners' power relationships and identities in activities where reading and writing were required. Employing the concept of 'figured worlds' (Holland *et al*, 1998), the focus of the discussions is on how this notion enhances the understanding of power relationships and identities in literacy practices. The book illustrates how literacy identities and power relationships of some local community members continuously varied from one context to another and in some cases, even within the same context. Using notions such as agency, artefact, resistance and positioning, it demonstrates the potential of the concept of figured worlds in addressing some fundamental questions raised within the NLS – especially those concerning power and identity. It also illustrates how an ethnographic approach to the study adult literacy enriches our understanding of not only what literacy means to the learners but also how and when they use it in their lived worlds.

Background to the National Adult Literacy Programme in Malawi

To begin with, it should be noted that virtually no Malawian local language has a single word to refer to literacy. For instance, in Chichewa, the country's national language, a descriptive phrase *kulemba ndi kuwerenga* (writing and reading[1]) is frequently used. Similarly, in Ciyawo, the language spoken in the area where my study was conducted, the words *kulemba ni kuŵalanga* are used. As such, in Chichewa the literate and 'illiterate' persons are referred to as *odziwa kulemba ndi kuwerenga* (literally, the able to write and read) and *osadziwa kulemba ndi kwerenga* (the not able to write and read) respectively.

Malawi's NALP dates back to as early as the colonial period. But a major shift in the history of the NALP took place when the Mponela Mass Education Pilot Project was launched in 1947 with an aim of exploring 'how to raise the standards of living and the betterment of the way of life of African communities' (Ministry of Women and Child Development, 2008: 3). However, due to various challenges such as poor management, lack of trained instructors and inadequate follow-up materials (Mpheluka, 1983), the project made little progress, and by 1949, it was discontinued. Meanwhile, another initiative called Community

---

[1] The Chichewa phrase usually begins with writing followed by reading.

Development Scheme was started in the same year at Domasi. But by 1953, this initiative, too, was terminated due to the same problems that led to the closure of the Mponela project.

In 1966 the Malawi government established a National Literacy Committee with a mandate to manage matters concerning literacy but still not much progress was made. Following this state of affairs, the Malawi government, with the assistance from UNESCO, launched another adult literacy initiative in 1967 (see Mipando and Higgs, 1982). It was as a result of the evaluation of this initiative that the Malawi government initiated and conducted a pilot functional literacy project with the assistance of UNESCO and UNDP from 1981 to 1985 resulting in the launch, in 1986, of the current Malawi National Functional Adult Literacy Programme.

Broadly, the goal of the NALP was 'to make approximately two million illiterate adults functionally literate by 1995 out of an estimated 3.6 million adult illiterates' (Ministry of Women and Children Affairs and Community Services, n.d.: 3). According to the Ministry, the programme specifically sought to accomplish the following objectives.

- To assist in achieving government development objectives by enabling rural populations to take advantage of modern and effective farming techniques to increase their overall productivity; attain improved health habits and practices; better family life and community living and foster national integration through education;
- To increase the attainment and use of literacy skills and sustain the process of learning and lifelong education for rural adults;
- To improve the status, general knowledge and technical skills of rural people especially smallholder farmers by making them receptive to innovations and modernization.

The NALP in Malawi targets non-literate adults aged fifteen and above. According to Rokadiya (1986: 4), 'priority is … given to those youths and adults – men and women … who are residing in rural areas; who are engaged in agriculture and allied occupations; who are smallholder farmers, housewives, parents and responsible members of the country'. These men and women undergo a ten months' literacy learning process covering reading, writing, numeracy and what is known as 'functional' content (ibid). Rokadiya notes further that the focus of the new programme was not only on literacy skills but also on linking literacy and development. Thus, 'the content of the literacy programme is to be based on the learning interests and needs of adults as well as development objectives' (ibid: 3).

In terms of literacy attainment, the NALP recognizes three levels. These levels are based on the assumed complexity of the reading and writing as well as the numeracy tasks involved. Rokadiya (ibid) outlines these levels as follows:

- Level I: The literacy learner is initiated to recognize written symbols. The learner can read and write some difficult and simple words in Chichewa and can also recognize, read and write mathematical signs.
- Level II: The literacy learner is able to read, comprehend and write correctly some Chichewa words, short simple sentences and a simple short paragraph. The learner can work out simple arithmetic problems.
- Level III: This is a stage at which the literacy learner demonstrates advanced skills in reading, writing and arithmetic. The learner can read and write comprehension questions of any simple passage and read and solve mathematical problems involving simple additions, subtractions, multiplications and divisions.

The government's commitment to the NALP was propelled by the keen interest the then life president had in the programme who believed that literacy was one of the 'weapons' which would help the country to defeat his three professed enemies, namely poverty, ignorance and disease.

Running through the literacy discourses of the time were metaphors of war whereby ignorance, poverty and disease were presented as if they were physical entities that should be fought and annihilated. At the same time, the government appeared to assume that literacy had an intrinsic capacity to conquer the professed enemies.

However, out of the three enemies, it is ignorance that dominated the government's literacy discourses. The names given to the government adult literacy programmes since independence reflect that tendency. The literacy initiatives that were delivered in the 1960s and 1970s ran under the *Ukani* Traditional Literacy Programme (Jeke, 2006). These programmes employed a series of books whose title was *Ukani* which could literally be translated as 'you wake up'. The current NALP, which was launched in 1986, is called *sukulu za kwacha* which literally means 'schools of daybreak'.

To some extent, both *ukani* and *sukulu za kwacha* are pejorative names. Both of them largely frame non-literate people as being ignorant, symbolized by their state of being *asleep* or being *in the dark*. In this context, literacy is portrayed as the light that would help the learners to be aware of what is happening around them. This framing of literacy reflected the international policy discourses of the time. During this period countries in the North tended to employ literacy metaphors that portrayed them as '"bringing light into darkness" or of "curing ills"' (Street & Lefstein, 2007: 225). These metaphors are evidently echoed by the self-proclaimed UNESCO Expert in Adult Literacy, Nasution (1969), who declares that

> ILLITERACY has been regarded as an enemy and evil which keeps people in darkness, bound to their traditions and superstitions; makes people resistant to change and new ideas, and isolated from progress, thus unaware and incapable of meeting the demands of their changing environment and ever-progressing world.
> (p. 6; original emphasis)

On the basis of these perceived ills of 'illiteracy', Nasution (ibid) claims that 'illiteracy' 'acts as a brake to development' (p. 7). In general, these discourses and metaphors suggest that non-literate people are arrogant, backward, ignorant and superstitious and because they are assumed to have these perceived malaises, they impede development. Such perceptions make some literacy experts in Malawi use language which portray non-literate people as offenders who require some form of sanctions. These experts bemoan 'the present status quo [which] allows illiterates to go on with life [thereby making] the need for literacy a fallacy' (Phiri & Safaraoh, 2003: xi).

Why literacy matters in Malawi: Policy perspectives

The Malawi government claims that its initiative to reduce poverty as outlined in the Malawi Poverty Reduction Strategy (MPRS) cannot be implemented successfully without paying attention to what it considers to be 'the illiteracy problem' (Ministry of Gender, Child Welfare and Community Services, 2004). The government is critical about the high 'illiteracy' rate arguing that it is one of the major challenges in almost all key socio-economic sectors of the country (Malawi Government, 2012).

The government's underlying assumption is that non-literate people cannot understand and do different development tasks owing to their assumed 'illiteracy'. This assumption dominates the adult literacy discourse in Malawi such that one of the objectives of the NALP is to, among other things, make rural people, mainly the smallholder farmers, 'receptive to innovations and modernisation' (Ministry of Women and Children Affairs and Community Services, n.d.: p. 4).

In this case, the government employs labels and metaphors such as 'rural people', 'smallholder farmers' and 'modernisation' and links 'illiteracy' with 'rurality' on the one hand and 'literacy' with 'modernity' on the other. The underlying message is that it is the rural people who have deficits in terms of knowledge and technical skills and that this situation can only be addressed by changing their mindset through literacy. In other words, it is assumed that 'the more literate people are, the more willing they are to accept and work for improvements in their societies' (Oxenham, 1980: 51).

When the government launched the Mponela Mass Education Pilot Project in 1947, its goal was to improve the living standards of the people of Malawi (Mipando & Higgs, 1982). In this way, the government discursively aligned the literacy initiative to UNDP's human development perspectives which place more emphasis on 'enlarging people's choices' (UNDP, 1990). This approach to development perceives the poor people in poor countries as the problem due to their perceived attitudes of resistance towards change (Rogers, 2004). The focus, therefore, becomes that of helping people to do things they were not able to do before (ibid). This is echoed in the goals of the NALP in Malawi referred to earlier where the government projects literacy as a means to improve the rural people's ability to produce more. Thus, non-literate people are portrayed as 'capital goods for commodity production' (UNDP, 1990: 11).

In the Draft National Adult Literacy Policy, the Malawi government reifies literacy as 'the core engine'. This policy framing is informed by the development discourse of poverty alleviation which the Malawi government adopted 'as its central operative development philosophy guiding all its development activities in the short, medium and long-term' (Government of the Republic of Malawi, 2007: 3). One of the approaches advocated by the MPRS is 'an emphasis on smallholder agriculture, to raise the productivity and income of the rural poor' (Government of Malawi, 2000: 10). The key assumption is that literacy will help in not only enabling the rural poor access information and technical innovations but also in making them accept and use such knowledge. It is further assumed that when the poor people's 'undesired' mindset is successfully changed, then their productivity will improve leading to a reduction in their poverty levels. Although it makes no distinction between literacy and education, the MPRS claims that 'adults who complete at least standard 8 are likely *not* to be poor' (Malawi Government, 2002: 7; original emphasis). It singles out the reduction of the 'illiteracy' rate as one of the major targets in the Malawi government's medium-term goal for poverty reduction. Similar links are also made by the Ministry of Education Science and Technology (2008) which states that 'literate people understand and easily follow instructions for performing various development activities' (p. 7). At the same time, the Malawi Growth and Development Strategy II (2012) is critical about the high 'illiteracy' rate, saying it is one of the major challenges in almost all key socio-economic sectors of the country (Malawi Government, 2012).

At the heart of all this is the thinking that development is a process of change from what are considered to be 'traditional' ways to those that are regarded as advanced and 'modern' practices. Such perceptions are entrenched not only in the goals, discourses and approaches of the NALP in Malawi but also in some of the stories in the primer. The stories are written in the manner that denigrate the assumed local knowledge systems which the literacy learners are perceived to possess and glorify 'modern' practices which the programme assumes they lack as evidenced in the translated story which follows.

This is not a Good Eating Practice

At Mr. Masina's household when they have chicken for a meal, children are not happy. Food is prepared early. Parents eat the '**delicious**' parts. Children are given chicken feet and the head. The parts with **lots of meat** are kept for the husband. Children know that in the evening they will eat **leftovers**.

Parents, this is not a good practice.

Children are required to eat the right type of food. It is not good for children to eat together with old people because they do not eat enough. Children must eat separately from old people. Parents, we should not forbid children from eating eggs. Eggs are important for our children to grow fast.

Source: *Chuma ndi Moyo* (2014) Lesson 12.

The structure of this story epitomizes the assumption underlying the NALP in Malawi regarding the state of knowledge and practices non-literate people have and do and what it expects them to be and do upon completion of the literacy lessons.

The story begins by providing the 'inappropriate' practice which presumably typifies what the adult literacy learners know and do (first four lines). Then the narrator of the story not only disqualifies the assumed inappropriate eating practice but also changes their role in the story. That is, they change from being just a narrator to an adjudicator by passing a judgement directed not just at the Masina family but at all parents in general, which presumably include the adult literacy learners (line standing alone).

The statement of disqualification is followed by what are regarded to be appropriate 'modern' practices of eating which the literacy learners ought to learn and adopt (last four lines). In other words, the wrong practices have to be erased from the literacy learners' minds through the adoption of the seemingly culturally neutral practices which are somewhat universally acceptable and are regarded as being 'modern'.

However, the Malawi government appears to use of the term 'modernity' as if it were a neutral and, therefore, an uncontested concept. But as Willis (2005: 2) postulates, modernity has both spatial and temporal dimensions such that 'what is "modern" in one place may be "old-fashioned" elsewhere'. I may also add that what was considered old-fashioned years ago may gain some significance and become modern now. Perhaps this is why some scholars such as Escobar (1995) construe development as a discourse. Escobar (ibid) argues that looking at development from a discursive point of view 'makes it possible to maintain the focus on domination' (pp. 5–6). Such a focus is crucial because 'in different ways, discursively, some people are empowered to know and decide, others to implement the decisions, yet others not to speak, or not to be heard if they do' (Hobart, 1993: 16). In other words, like literacy, 'the field of activity known as "development"' (Rogers, 2004: 13) is also imbued with power relations.

As such, most 'development writing constantly delineates and divides territory [and people] by means of a relentless dualistic logic' (Crush, 1995: 14). There is always a distinction between those that are deemed to be doing well and therefore do not require change anymore and those that need assistance to change. So we have labels such as 'First World' and 'Third World', 'traditional' and 'modern', 'developed' and 'underdeveloped', 'affluent' and the 'poor', 'literate' and 'illiterate' among others. Given these labels, it is the 'Third World', the 'traditional', the 'underdeveloped', the 'poor' or the 'illiterate' that need to change. Thus, all the debates on what constitutes development appear to suggest that 'development implies change, affecting most, if not all areas of life' (Kingsbury, 2004: 12).

The instrumental views of literacy running through the official documents referred to in the sections above parallel those expressed in some international declarations to which Malawi assented. The World Conference on Education for All (WCEFA) Inter-Agency Commission (1990: 36) considers literacy programmes as being essential because on the one hand literacy is important in itself and on the other it is the basis of other skills needed in life (see also Dakar Framework of Action in UNESCO, 2000). The commission notes further that '*literacy is* a life skill and the primary learning tool for personal and community development and self-sufficiency in a rapidly changing and increasingly interdependent world' (p. 63; original emphasis).

Conclusion

While many scholars and experts have adopted new ways of conceptualizing literacy elsewhere, in Malawi literacy continues to be viewed as a set of tangible skills which some citizens have and others lack. As a result, the bulk of the literacy studies conducted in the country aim at understanding ways that would help in making Malawians presumed to be non-literate learn the government's privileged literacy and not at exploring how different literacies facilitate or constrain the people's participation in various activities where such literacies are required.

At the heart of the NALP in Malawi is the belief that literacy as defined by the government can bring about social change. Thus, 'traditional knowledge' is not valued while 'modernity' is reified although what constitutes 'traditional' or 'modernity' is rarely stated. This book seeks to illustrate how exploring power and identity in literacy practices enriches the understanding of literacy as a social practice. Employing Holland *et al*'s (1998) notion of figured world, the book shows how fluid community members' identities were and how power relationships narrowed their space to learn the literacies they desired.

2

Power and Identity: Exploring Theoretical Perspectives

In this chapter, I examine the conceptual tools I am using in this book to account for the literacy practices which some of the community members of Sawabu village encountered in their lived worlds. In Chapter 1, I noted that the conceptualization of literacy has shifted from viewing it as a standalone and tangible skill to perceiving it as a social practice. I begin this chapter by providing a brief account of this theory and its critique on power followed by a discussion on Holland *et al*'s (1998) theory of self and identity, especially the concept of figured world. My aim is to tease out possible ways in which the conceptual tools discussed can be used together as lenses through which the literacy practices encountered by the community members in Sawabu village can be understood. Specifically, I explore how issues of power and identity in literacy practices can be dealt with by complementing the social theory of literacy with the notion of figured world.

The social theory of literacy

The social theory of literacy was first developed in the 1980s (Papen, 2005) by scholars who came from a range of disciplines such as anthropology (Street, 1984), history (Graff, 1979), psychology (Scribner & Cole, 1981) and sociolinguistics (Heath, 1983; Gee, 1987; Baynham, 1995). They did not subscribe to the 'traditional psychological approach to literacy' in which literacy was perceived as a 'cognitive phenomenon' understood from the point of view of 'mental states and mental processing' (Gee, n.d.: 2). Instead, their focus was on the role literacy played in people's everyday life (Papen, 2005). The work of these researchers laid the foundation of what is now known as the New Literacy Studies (NLS). According to Street (2003: 77):

> what has come to be termed the 'New Literacy Studies' (NLS) (…) represents a new tradition in considering the nature of literacy, focusing not so much on acquisition of skills, as in dominant approaches, but rather on what it means to think of literacy as a social practice.

Following this paradigm shift, in contemporary literacy studies a distinction is generally made between what Street (1993) calls an autonomous model of literacy on the one hand, and the ideological one on the other. The autonomous model of literacy 'works from the assumption that literacy in itself, autonomously, will have effects on other social and cognitive practices' (Street, 2001: 7). In this model, literacy is usually seen as a technical skill which involves coding and decoding letters, and which, once mastered by an individual, can be used by them anywhere it is required. The key assumption underpinning this model is that literacy is neutral and the same anywhere.

By contrast, the ideological model looks at 'literacy practices as inextricably linked to cultural and power structures in society, and recognize the variety of cultural practices associated with reading and writing in different contexts' (Street, 1993: 7). Literacy is tied to the activities people do. In fact, it is 'something people do; it is an activity, located in the space between thought and text' (Barton & Hamilton, 1998: 3). Besides, literacy is never neutral but rather always influenced by our own points of view. Crucially, literacy is 'always contextualised, situated within a particular socio-cultural setting' (Rogers *et al*, 1999: 55).

At the heart of the social theory of literacy are two key concepts, namely literacy events and literacy practices. When we talk about literacy events, we are essentially referring to 'what people do with reading and writing: they are the uses of literacy, which can be observed and described' (Papen, 2005: 31; see also St. Clair, 2010). Viewed in this way, 'the notion of events stresses the situated nature of literacy, that it always exists in a social context' (Barton & Hamilton, 1998: 7). But as Papen (2003) observes, the notion of literacy event is essentially descriptive compared to the concept of literacy practices which

> moves us into the realm of analysis trying to understand the meanings of events observed, looking for patterns across events, similarities and differences between them and trying to understand their relationship with other elements of the world.
> (p. 31)

Thus, the concept of literacy practices is not only broader but also more inclusive and, as Papen notes, it takes us further into analysis. Street (2003) emphasizes this when he says

> I have employed the phrase "literacy practices" (…) as a means of focusing upon "social practices and conceptions of reading and writing", although I later elaborated the term to take into account both "events" in Heath's sense and of the social models of literacy that participants bring to bear upon those events and that give meaning to them …
>
> (p. 78)

However, my reading of the work done by NLS scholars seems to suggest that they differ slightly, not only in the way they articulate the two notions but also in the choices they make when employing them in their writings. Thus, a number of literacy scholarly works from the Literacy Research Group, Lancaster University (Barton & Ivanič 1991; Barton & Hamilton 1998; Hamilton, Barton & Ivanič 1994; Ivanič 1997) have largely employed the notion of literacy event (Street, 2000), whereas Street's work has mostly emphasized literacy practices. Their differences in backgrounds, language and linguistics for the Lancaster group and anthropology for Street, may explain these scholars' preferences in the choice and use of the two terms.

Despite these minor differences, the NLS scholars, regardless of their orientation, seem to be moving towards building a consensus on what literacy event and literacy practices are. For instance, Barton and Hamilton (1998) make a clear distinction between literacy events and literacy practices by suggesting that the former are tangible and therefore observable, while the latter are not. To some extent, Street (2000: 21) also appears to share this view when he says, 'you can photograph literacy events but you cannot photograph literacy practices'.

But Street's (2003) characterization of literacy practices cited earlier appears to subsume literacy event. He explains that

> the concept of literacy practices does, I think, attempt to handle the events and the patterns of activity around literacy but to *link* them to something broader of a cultural and social kind
>
> (Street, 2000: 21, original emphasis).

Viewed in this way, literacy practices become dual in nature, that is, they are both visible and invisible (Cheffy, 2008) and this is how I employ the term in this book. Conceptualizing literacy practices in this dual model allows me not only to describe what the community members do with reading and writing but also to explore their discourses and meanings of literacy. As Barton and Papen observe, 'taken together, the terms event and practice are key units of analysis which link theory and methodology and which have proved useful in understanding reading and writing' (2010: 11).

Apart from the notions of literacy event and literacy practices, the social theory of literacy gives texts some prominence. Hence, any 'study of literacy is partly a study of texts and how they are produced and used' (Barton & Hamilton, 1998: 8). This is the case because social practices, of which literacy is a part, are mediated by texts (Barton, 2009). However, although I agree in principle on the centrality of texts in literacy studies, in this book I prefer to use the term artefact because it is a broader concept 'of which texts are a significant category' (Hamilton, 2016: 8). (I discuss the notion of artefact later in this chapter).

Another notion which has gained much attention in NLS is that of mediation. According to Thompson (2015: 481) 'literacy mediation is often a means by which socially and economically disadvantaged groups can gain access to discourses of power.' In other words, it allows individuals who are assumed to be non-literate to participate in activities which require reading and writing by getting support from others. In most cases 'the genres or codes that are being sought out in the mediation process, derive from the dominant culture and its institutions' (ibid). In Chapter 4, I will be using this notion to understand how non-literate community members at Sawabu village navigated through activities in which reading and writing were required.

As I mentioned earlier, although the social theory of literacy has been embraced by many researchers and scholars, it has at the same time generated many debates and controversies (see Brandt & Clinton, 2002; Bartlett, 2008b; Maddox, 2008; Baynham & Prinsloo, 2009; Kell, 2009; St. Clair, 2010). In the section that foolows I look at 'the problems raised by it both in general theoretical terms and, more specifically, for practice in educational contexts' (Street, 2003: 79). Specifically, I highlight what some scholars perceive as the failure of the NLS in addressing the issues of power and identity in literacy practices.

Power and identity in new literacy studies: A brief critique

The social theory of literacy is faulted for not going far enough in articulating certain aspects of literacy practices, particularly power and identity that come into play in people's literacy-mediated social encounters. Papen (2005) observes that some of the difficulties likely to be experienced when approaching literacy programmes from a social practices model could – at least to a certain extent – result from the NLS failure to sufficiently theorize issues of power with regards to literacy.

(p. 15)

St. Clair (2010) and Collins and Blot (2003) highlight similar observations. St. Clair acknowledges the fact that the New Literacy Studies recognize power, only that 'the implications of these issues for the theorization of literacy seem to be quite underdeveloped' (p. 31). Also, although issues of power are subsumed in the ideological model, there is still lack of clarity with regard to 'power-in-literacy which captures the intricate ways in which power, knowledge and forms of subjectivity are interconnected with "uses of literacy"' in different contexts (Collins & Blot, 2003: 66). Street (1993) admits that identifying different literacy practices through ethnographic studies is not enough and calls for the need to have 'bold theoretical models that recognise the central role of power relations in literacy practices' (p. 2). In this book, I am using the social theory of literacy together with Holland *et al*'s (1998) theory of self and identity, especially the concept of figured world, to account for issues of power and identity in community members' lived worlds where literacy had a role.

Figured world, or is it 'As If Realms?'

Holland *et al* (1998) claim that 'the conceptual importance of figured worlds has been emphasized in anthropology for some time' (p. 54). They cite the works of Hallowell (1955a), Shweder (1991) and Quinn and Holland (1987) to support their claim. According to these scholars Hallowell contends that human beings live in culturally defined worlds and that they understand themselves relative to those worlds; they call such worlds 'behavioural environments'. Similarly, they cite the psychological anthropologist Shweder who talks about such environments as 'intentional worlds'. On their part, Quinn and Holland discuss the 'taken for granted worlds that are culturally modelled', using a concept reminiscent of figured world which they call 'simplified worlds' (Holland *et al*, 1998: 55). What these citations suggest is that the underlying principle behind the conceptual framework of 'figured world' is not entirely new.

Figured world is one of what Holland *et al* (1998) call contexts for the production and reproduction of identity which, together with other contexts, constitute a broader sociocultural theory of self and identity. A figured world is 'a socially and culturally constructed realm of interpretation in which particular characters and actors are recognized, significance is assigned to certain acts, and particular outcomes are valued over others' (ibid: 52). This conceptualization of figured world covers a number of key issues worth paying attention to. First, the description suggests that 'social communities' (Lave & Wenger, 1991) and culture are key to the creation of the context from where the participants, their actions and the results of such actions derive their significance (I explain how I am using the terms 'community' and 'culture' later in this chapter).

Second, not everyone is recognized in a figured world. For one to be recognized in a given context, they need to meet the expected requirements. Third, based on such requirements, what people do, including the outcomes of their acts, is also valued differently. This characterization of the concept of figured world mirrors adult literacy learning in Malawi. For example, as 'socially and culturally [organised] realm[s] of interpretation' (Holland *et al*, 1998: 52), adult literacy classes in Malawi involve actors who are recognized as 'illiterate adults aged 15 and above' (Ministry of Gender, Child Welfare and Community Services, 2005). From the government point of view, significance is given to the learning of 'functional knowledge' and the outcome that is valued most is social change. I am therefore using the concept of figured world to understand the learners' literacy practices as well as their participation in this context. My framing of the adult literacy learning and other social activities as figured worlds is based on my conviction that 'figured worlds are socially organized and reproduced; *they are like activities in the usual, institutional sense*' (ibid: 41, emphasis mine). Likening a figured world to social activities parallels the conceptualization of literacy as a social practice, especially when we view literacy as 'something people do; [that is], an activity, located in the space between thought and text' (Barton & Hamilton, 1998: 3). Holland *et al* (1998) explain that

> under the rubric of culturally figured worlds or figured worlds we include all those cultural realms peopled by characters from collective imaginings: academia, the factory, crime, romance, environmental activism ….
>
> (p. 51)

We can therefore, think of figured worlds as people's imagined areas of interests or activities, which are actualized in real life through various forms of engagement. We can talk about the figured worlds of factory, wedding, crime, romance and a figured world of adult literacy learning. In this regard, as a figured world, adult literacy learning is occupied by 'figures', 'characters' and 'types' who perform their requisite tasks and 'who also have styles of interacting within, distinguishable perspectives on, and orientations toward it' (p. 51). Thus, a figured world of adult literacy learning may 'include "functional illiterates," "good readers," and "illiterates" who struggle to become literate or demonstrate their literacy in a variety of settings including the classroom, the marketplace, and home' (Bartlett, 2002: 12).

What is interesting about the concept of figured world is that, like the social theory of literacy which conceptualizes literacy as being intertwined with power, figured worlds entail power. They revolve around positions of status and influence. They are 'social encounters in which participants' positions matter' (ibid). Consequently, 'some figured worlds we may never enter because of our social position or rank; some we may deny to others; some we may simply miss by contingency; some we may learn fully' (ibid: 41).

Central to the concept of figured world is the notion of cultural means. Each figured world is organized by '"cultural means" or narratives, storylines and other cultural genre ... ' (Urrieta Jr., 2007: 109). These narratives provide both the context for interpretation and 'cultural resources that are durable and socially reproduced' (ibid). For instance, Holland *et al* (1998) demonstrate how in the 'figured world of domestic relations', the meanings of characters, acts and events in the everyday life of women in Naudada in Nepal were constructed relative to a given storyline. In this case, to be a 'good woman' one was assumed to have a given life path. Though not prescriptive, the storyline provided a background against which women and men, their acts and incidences were interpreted in this figured world. It provided the cultural means by which the 'figured world of domestic relations' was organized. Holland *et al* (1998: 55) view cultural schemas or cultural models as 'stereotypical distillates, generalizations from past experience that people make'. To some extent, cultural means are not necessarily truths in a scientific sense, but rather they are some regularities that become solidified over time to be taken as the norm (ibid).

Gee (1999, 2005, 2011) appears to conceptualize cultural means, which he prefers to call discourse models/figured worlds, in the same way. He (2005) defines discourse models as 'simplified, often unconscious and taken-for-granted, theories about how the world works that we use to get on efficiently with our daily lives' (p. 71). Just like Holland *et al*, Gee claims that these discourse models are learnt from past experiences ' ... but, crucially, as these experiences are shaped and normed by the social and cultural groups to which we belong' (ibid). We use such experiences to deduce what we think is 'normal' ' ... and tend to act on these assumptions unless something clearly tells us that we are facing an exception' (ibid).

In this book, the use of the term 'figured world' is reserved to characterize the contexts of meaning making as postulated by Holland *et al* (1998) to minimize any confusion. In the same way, I restrict the use of the term cultural means/cultural schema/cultural models to refer to the 'typical stories' (Gee, 2011: 70). During my fieldwork, I heard stories reminiscent of those narrated in a very different figured world of Alcoholics Anonymous in the United States as reported by Holland *et al* (1998). Some community members told me their experiences with literacy prior to and after enrolling for the literacy lessons to demonstrate to me the significance of their literacy lessons. Therefore, I employ the notion of cultural means to interrogate such stories with a view to understanding community members' literacy practices. In addition, I employ this notion to explore community members' participation in some of their lived worlds.

Figured world and domain

The social theory of literacy which I discussed earlier characterizes people's varied contexts of activity as domains. Barton and Hamilton (2000: 11) define domain as 'structured, patterned contexts within which literacy is used and learned'. My understanding of the characterization of both domains and figured worlds suggests that they somewhat differ in how the contexts are distinguished as well as in scope. In terms of distinguishing, I have the impression that domain emphasizes demarcating 'areas of social activity' (Papen, 2002; see Barton & Hamilton, 2000) while figured world stresses on meaning-making. As far as scope is concerned, I note that domain tends to be broad and generally not as elastic as figured world. Figured world is about how people construct, shape and interact with such worlds. For instance, home, education (school), work place and religion (church/mosque) are sometimes cited as examples of domains (see Barton & Hamilton, ibid).

However, if we take the church as an example, we note that it has different activities that require acts and actors that are figured differently. A Christian Church wedding, for example, would require a bride, a bridegroom, best man, bride's maids and other actors in many contexts. It would also require artefacts such as rings, veils and wedding dresses of particular colours. Particular acts such as the exchanging of rings and vows would be given significance and particular literacy practices would be recognized. Although the figuring of weddings may differ from one church to the other, some of the generic acts, actors and artefacts cited here set weddings apart from funeral ceremonies and prayer sermons. In this case, wedding, funeral ceremonies and prayer sermons can be seen as different figured worlds evoked by particular artefacts and each of them may have underlying cultural models. What this suggests is that although church may equally be perceived as a figured world in the same way as we do with domain, the concept of figured world allows us to see finer figured worlds within broader ones. Needless to say that, just as we have 'questions of the permeability of boundaries, of leakages and movement between boundaries, and of overlap between domains' (Barton & Hamilton, 2000: 11), the same is the case with figured worlds. Holland *et al* (1998) acknowledge the 'embedding of activities' as being 'central to an understanding of figured worlds', citing how 'the world of romance and attractiveness plays a prominent role in the production and reproduction of gender privilege in the United States' as an example (p. 57).

Agency, objectification and improvisation in figured worlds

In characterizing identities in figured worlds, Holland *et al* (1998) pay attention to what the actors do in these worlds. The authors perceive objectification as 'representations' or 'visions' with a potential to 'motivate (plans for) action, sometimes even life-changing action' (p. 142). They claim that

> these objectifications become the organizing basis of resentment and often of more active resistance. When individuals learn about figured worlds and come, in some sense, to identify themselves in those worlds, their participation may include reactions to the treatment they have received as occupants of the positions figured by the worlds.
>
> (p. 143)

What this suggests is that in figured worlds, identities are not fixed and stable. They are prone to being negotiated whenever required. In fact, Holland *et al* (ibid) state that people use the same tools they had adopted to guide the behaviour that was required to 'reproduce structures of privilege and the identities, dominant and subordinate, defined within them' to liberate themselves from 'the social environment' (ibid). Viewed in this way, I would say that objectification provides individuals with some form of agency, especially when one visualizes a representation he or she finds undesirable. Citing Inden (1990), Holland *et al* (ibid) describe human agency as

> the realized capacity of people to act upon their world and not only to know about or give personal or intersubjective significance to it. That capacity is the power of people to act purposively and reflectively, in more or less complex interrelationships with one another, to reiterate and remake the world in which they live, in circumstances where they may consider different courses of action possible and desirable, though not necessarily from the same point of view.
>
> (p. 42)

Understood in this way, I would argue that figured worlds are to some extent contexts of power struggle. With this agency, people can challenge decisions and actions as well as contest their social positioning in their lived worlds. Holland *et al* (ibid) note that these disruptions happen not only at individual level but also 'on the collective level as well' (p. 141).

As regards improvisations, Holland *et al* (1998: 17–18) describe them as 'the sort of impromptu actions that occur when our past, brought to the present as *habitus,* meets with a particular combination of circumstances and conditions for which we have no set response' (original emphasis). These improvisations provide the means for change in that once effected they become a new norm.

Positionality

Positionality is another context for the production and reproduction of identity which is part of Holland *et al*'s (1998) broader theory of self and identity. When we talk about positionality, we mean 'the positions "offered" to people in different figured worlds …' (Urrieta Jr., 2007: 111). It refers to 'the fact that personal activity (…) always occurs from a particular place in a social field of ordered and interrelated points or positions of possible activity' (Holland *et al*, 1998: 44). These positions are not necessarily physical spaces, rather they involve 'entitlement to social and material resources and so to the higher deference, respect, and legitimacy accorded to those genders, races, ethnic groups, castes, and sexualities privileged by society' (ibid: 271). The authors claim that whenever we take part in social life or activity, we are assumed to take a particular perspective. Viewed from the point of view of discursive practices, we can describe positioning as the 'process whereby selves are located in conversation as observably and subjectively coherent participants in jointly produced story lines' (Davies & Harré, 2007: n.p.). As such, each discursive practice has some constitutive force that lies 'in its provision of subject position' (ibid). Therefore,

> once having taken up a particular position as one's own, a person inevitably sees the world from the vantage point of that position and in terms of the particular images, metaphors, story lines and concepts which are made relevant within the particular discursive practice in which they are positioned.
>
> (ibid)

Davies and Harré (2007) primarily focus on conversations in their discussion of the concept of positioning and they employ the term 'positioning' to understand personhood. They identify two forms of positioning, namely interactive and reflexive. By interactive positioning they mean, 'what one person says positions the other', whereas in reflexive positioning 'one positions oneself' (ibid). They posit that 'among the products of discursive practices are the very persons who engage in them' (ibid). In Chapter 5, I adapt Davies and Harré's perspectives of discursive positionality to explore the subject positions that were available to community members both in oral and written texts.

Exploring positionality is crucial, bearing in mind that 'persons look at the world from the positions into which they are persistently cast' (Holland *et al*, 1998: 44). Besides, 'people tell others who they are, but even more important, they tell themselves and then try to act as though they are who they say they are' (Holland *et al*, 1998: 3). Therefore, first, there is need to understand what subject positions were available to the literacy learners in some of the literacy-mediated activities they participated in. Second, it is imperative to examine the extent to which these subject positions facilitated community members' learning and uses of literacy.

Related to the context of positionality is that of authoring. Holland *et al* (1998) contend that people must provide a response to the world, and therefore they conceptualize authorship as 'a matter of orchestration: of arranging the identifiable social discourses/practices that are one's resources … in order to craft a response in a time and space defined by others' standpoints in activity … ' (p. 272). What this implies is that in any context, we bring with us multiple discourses and practices which we draw on and arrange in order to either accept, reject or negotiate our identity. In this regard, 'authorship is not a choice' (ibid) because even 'a non-response is also a type of response' (Urrieta, Jr., 2007: 111). In Chapter 5, I am using this lens to examine how some literacy learners drew on their social discourses and practices to redefine their literacy identities to enrol or to opt out from English literacy lessons.

Artefacts and figured worlds

In my discussion on the social theory of literacy, I stated my preference of the term artefact over that of texts to designate the items some community members employed in some of their social activities where literacy had a role. Thus, while the ration cards which some community members used to get relief food at the food distribution centres can be designated as either text or artefact, the inkpads which others employed to acknowledge receipt of the food items can only be characterized as artefacts. In this regard, the notion of artefact provides the opportunity to explore and take some community members' literacy experiences beyond speech and written word.

Paying attention to such artefacts is crucial because 'artifacts are the means by which figured worlds are evoked, collectively developed, individually learned, and made socially and personally powerful' (Holland *et al*, 1998: 61). Therefore, to understand the figured world of adult literacy learning, I characterize various documents and items which the community members encountered in this context as artefacts. Likewise, I conceptualize the materials such as pens and ink pads, which they employed to facilitate their participation in other lived worlds, as artefacts. The significance of these materials cannot be overstated, since 'artifacts are social constructions or products of human activity, and they in turn may become tools engaged in processes of cultural production' (Bartlett, 2002: 13). It is in this way that 'artifacts such as pronouns and chips evoke the worlds to which they are relevant, and position individuals with respect to those worlds' (Holland *et al*, ibid: 63). Crucially, 'people learn to ascribe meaning to artifacts such as objects, events, discourses, and to people as understood in relation to particular figured worlds' (Urrieta Jr., 2007: 110). Holland *et al* (1998) inform us that in our lives, artefacts are very important because they are capable of changing our perception, cognition and affection. In this book, my focus is not only on understanding what the community members thought about the artefacts they came across in various social encounters, but also on how they felt when they used them. I also explore whether or not such artefacts promoted or constrained their participation in some of their lived worlds.

Towards conceptualizing power and identities

Lukes (2007) observes that 'the concept of power is essentially contested' (p. 83). He argues that both the definition and use of the term are inseparably tied to a given set of value assumptions. It may not be surprising therefore that different scholars conceptualize power differently. For instance, Wenger (1998) sees power as 'a condition for the possibility of socially organized action' (p. 180). He sees power as being 'inherent in social life' (p. 191). Wenger appears not to view power as a 'commodity' which some people can or cannot possess. He characterizes it 'primarily as the ability to act in line with the enterprises we pursue … ' (ibid). As such, power 'becomes apparent when it is exercised' (Townley, 1993: 520). On his part, Lukes (2005) theorizes power as manifesting 'two distinct variants … "power to" and "power over," where the latter is a subspecies of the former' (p. 69). 'Power to' 'indicates a "capacity", a "facility", an "ability"' (ibid: 34).

With regard to 'power over', it is both 'relational and asymmetrical' and, therefore 'to have power is to have power over another or others' (ibid: 73). It is not my intention to attempt to exhaust all definitions and dimensions or forms of this highly contested concept within this limited space. Besides, I do not intend to engage myself in any argument concerning which conceptualization is defensible or not but rather I just want to indicate how power is understood in this book.

In Chapter 6, I discuss the dilemmas which both the literacy learners and their instructors had in decision making at Sawabu literacy centre. Their failure to suspend literacy lessons without the approval of officers at the district office, for example, can be understood as the district officers having power over the instructors and their literacy learners in decision making processes. In short, I am using Lukes's understanding of power together with Holland *et al*'s (1998) concepts of agency, resistance and improvisation to account for the voices that were privileged or muted in decision-making at this literacy class.

Just like power, the term 'identity' is also subject to multiple interpretations and it would be naïve for me to venture into any assumed justifiable and reasonable review of literature on this subject. As I said in Chapter 1, my aim in this book is demonstrate how Holland *et al*'s theory of self and identity, particularly the notion of figured world, can be useful in understanding power and identity in literacy practices.

Holland *et al* (1998) view identities as 'self-understandings, especially those with strong emotional resonance' (p. 3). It is through identity that we care for and care about whatever is taking place around us. In other words, identities are 'very important bases from which people create new activities, new worlds, and new ways of being' (ibid: 5). These scholars build their theory of identity from the proposition that 'identities are lived in and through activity and so must be conceptualised as they develop in social practice'. This premise parallels the current views of literacy as a social practice in which it is understood that 'literacies, like other uses of language, entail social identities' (Bartlett, 2005: 2). This seems to suggest that identity is not only discursive and situated but that it is also somewhat implicated in people's behaviour.

Holland *et al* (1998) make it clear that their conceptualization of identity is a blend of two perspectives. On the one hand, drawing on the work of Bakhtin, they frame identity as being dialogic and on the other, based on the work of Vygotsky, they characterize identity as being developmental. In this way Holland *et al* (ibid) aim 'to build upon and move beyond two central approaches – the culturalist and the constructivist – to understand people's actions and possibilities' (p. 8).

The authors see identity as being both 'positional' and 'figurative'. According to them, positional (relational) identity is

> a person's apprehension of her social position in a lived world: that is depending on the others present, of her greater or lesser access to spaces, activities, genres, and, through those genres, authoritative voices, or any voice at all.
>
> (ibid: 127–8)

Characterized in this way, positional identities can therefore be viewed as 'self-understandings' evoked through participation in a social activity. Hence,

> positional identities have to do with the day-to-day and on the ground relations of power, deference and entitlements, social affiliation and distance – with the social-interactional, social-relational structures of the lived world.
>
> (ibid: 127)

In short, 'positional identities are about acts that constitute relations of hierarchy, distance or perhaps affiliation' (ibid: 128). With regard to figurative identities, Holland *et al* view them as 'the stories, acts and characters that make the world a cultural world' (ibid). Figurative identities 'are about signs that evoke storylines or plots among generic characters' (ibid).

Community and culture in this book

In my discussions of the concept of figured world earlier, I mentioned two terms which will be used extensively in this book namely, community and culture. The two terms need a brief discussion because they too are subject to multiple interpretations. When Anderson (1991: 6) asserts that 'all communities larger than primordial villages of face to face contact (…) are imagined', it appears to make sense to me. When he goes further and contends that 'communities are to be distinguished, not by their falsity/genuineness, but by the style in which they are imagined' (ibid), the case seems to be settled.

However, my reading of literature on this term suggests that it is 'highly elusive, with numerous competing interpretations' (Kepe, 1999: 418). According to Delanty (2003), scholars from a range of disciplines differ in the use of the term prompting others 'to question its usefulness' (p. 2). Notwithstanding this, Delanty (ibid) provides a glimpse of what community may entail, saying 'the term *community* does in fact designate both an idea about belonging and a particular social phenomenon, such as expressions of longing for community, the search for meaning and solidarity, and collective identities' (p. 3). Plant (1974), cited in Gereluk (2006), also appears to acknowledge that the term 'community' is linked not only 'to identity of functional interests, to a sense of belonging, to shared cultural and ethnic idea and values, to a way of life' but also 'to a locality' (p. 8). Without attempting to exhaust all possible descriptions and usage of the term or seeking its universally accepted definition, I am using the term to principally designate 'a particular form of social organisation based on small groups, such as neighbourhoods, the small town, or a spatially bounded locality' (Delanty, 2003: 2). Thus, I am using the term 'community' to refer to 'people who share a common locality' (Kepe, 1999: 419, citing Selznick, 1996). I frame community in this manner because I agree that defining community in terms of locality 'makes sense, as a practical matter, because residence is a congenial condition – perhaps the most congenial condition – for forming and sustaining community life' (Selznick, 1992: 359). However, just like Barton and Hamilton (1998) who realized that community as a term was far more complex than the geographical and social class boundaries they had designated, I had similar dilemmas which I discuss in Chapter 3. Hence my perception of the term community encompasses other factors such as 'concerted activity and shared belief' (Selznick, 1992: 359).

Street (2010) observes that one of the reasons why efforts to understand culture have faced some challenges is 'the desire to define it, or to say clearly what it is' (p. 581). He, therefore, advises against defining the term because 'we tend to believe the categories and definitions we construct in an essentialist way, as though we had thereby found out what culture is.' He argues that instead of looking for a definition of culture, we should focus our attention on 'what culture does' (ibid). He sees culture 'as a verb'. Thus, it is 'an active process of meaning making and contest over definition' (ibid). In the same vein, Holliday (1999: 247) perceives culture as 'the composite of cohesive behaviour within any social grouping ... ' The term is used in the sense of 'small culture' that focuses more on the 'activities taking place within the group than with the nature of the group itself' (ibid: 250). He says that 'ethnography uses small culture as a location for research, as an interpretive device for understanding emergent behaviour, rather than seeking to explain prescribed ethnic, national or international difference' (p. 237). In Chapter 6, I am using Holliday's perspectives to understand community members' interactions and experiences, especially at the literacy class.

Conclusion

The social theory of literacy continues to generate interest from literacy practitioners and scholars because it opens new and robust ways of conceptualizing literacy not just as a skill which people need to learn and use whenever required but also as something rooted in what people do. However, there are questions concerning the theory's adequacy, especially when researching power and identity in literacy practices. The major concern is that the theory does not explicitly provide conceptual tools to deal with such issues in literacy studies. However, as I stated earlier in this chapter, rather than looking at this 'inadequacy' as a problem, it is useful to perceive it as a window through which other theories can be brought in to complement the social theory of literacy. Using multiple theories to understand issues at hand is not an odd practice since, as Jørgensen and Phillips (2002) note elsewhere, when required it is permissible to combine perspectives because 'different perspectives provide different forms of knowledge about the phenomena so that, together, they produce a broader understanding' (p. 4).

3

'Being there': Dilemmas and Opportunities

The purpose of my study was to contribute theoretically, to the study of literacy as a social practice by exploring how the concept of figured world can help us to investigate and understand better the social and situated nature of literacy. To do this, I examined community members' literacy practices, discourses and meanings in some of their lived worlds to establish their literacy identities and power relationships. Realizing that this study was 'about the *practices of everyday life*, the way those practices are built out of shared knowledge, plus all the other things that are relevant to the moment' (Agar, 1996: 9; original emphasis), my strategy of enquiry was ethnography within a qualitative research design.

Becoming a community member

In Chapter 1, I indicated that my study was conducted at Sawabu village in Zomba, Malawi. I first arrived in Sawabu village on 9 September 2015, and I was very enthusiastic and keen on renting a house and staying in the village. This enthusiasm was propelled by my conviction that in order to know and understand the people's lived experiences, I had to be part of the community itself. I shared the view that ' … to know other humans the ethnographer must do as others do, live with others, eat, work and experience the same daily patterns as others' (Madden, 2010: 16). I explained my plan to the cluster supervisor. I wanted him to help me hunt for a vacant house that was habitable. But the news I got was not encouraging. He told me that there was a vacant house at one of the literacy learners' place, Ms Awali. However, he said that the place was not ideal for me because Ms Awali brewed and sold beer within her compound. The supervisor feared that Ms Awali's customers would be disturbing me. He further told me that the community was not safe, especially as the rainy season approached. He said that most of the young men who depended on brick moulding would have no source of income during this period and they resorted to stealing. They would easily monitor my movements and break into my rented house since they knew that I had a steady source of income.

As I took time to ponder over the cluster supervisor's observations, the literacy learners had their own stories revolving around the security of the community. I made a habit of going to the class early. The learners came in, one by one and found me already there sitting outside the classroom. As we waited for more learners to come, those present usually talked about various issues. It was on such occasions when I heard them talk about the security of the area in general, and their community in particular that their stories scared me even more.

Despite the security concerns, I still wanted to stay in the village. My only challenge was how to balance between my own safety and collecting adequate data for my study. As a compromise, I decided to rent a house where I could stay for some hours during the day before and after observing the classes. Although the supervisor had warned me about the disturbances at Ms Awali's place, I thought that this was the ideal place for me. My plan was that if I stayed at this place, I could easily interact with Ms Awali's customers regardless of whether they were drunk or not. But when I finally rented the house, some challenges emerged.

First, Ms Awali looked at my rented house as an office. Anytime her customers came close to me, she told them to leave me alone. I tried to assure her that I was comfortable chatting with the customers but she still found it difficult to let the customers socialize with me. Despite her objections, I occasionally had a chance of chatting with some of the customers. It was during such informal conversations that I identified some of my potential interviewees. It was also during such informal interactions that I came to realize how I was being perceived by some community members. Some of Ms Awali's customers came to ask me if I could buy land from them. Others came to ask if I could offer them employment at the place I was working. When I told them that I could not afford to pay for their land and that I did not have powers to employ anyone, they said that I was just pretending.

Second, apart from Ms Awali and her customers, no one except the cluster supervisor came to chat with me at my rented house. While I somehow understood the cultural complications that would prevent the women from coming to my rented house, it was rather difficult to comprehend why men behaved in the same way. Slowly, it emerged that the men associated me more with the literacy class than with the community at large. This perception emanated from the fact that people saw me more often at the literacy classroom than anywhere else. In fact, some of them called me the headmaster of the adult literacy centre.

These challenges aside, my decision to rent a house appeared to have served the purpose. By staying in the village, I had more opportunities to understand the lived experiences of the community members. I had a chance to hear stories I would otherwise have missed. Furthermore, it was easy for me to identify and arrange for in-depth discussions with some of the members of the community.

Research methods

It is customary that in order to conduct any research successfully, one needs appropriate research methods. In keeping with my understanding of ethnography 'as a set of methods' (Hammersley & Atkinson, 2007: 4), my study employed various research methods, namely participant observation, semi-structured and informal interviews, as well as focus group discussions (FGD). Other sources of information were documentation and photography.

Participant observation was employed in a number of contexts and activities in which the community members took part, one of them being the adult literacy class. During the early days, every time I went to the literacy class, the adult literacy learners had to go to the village headperson to borrow a chair for me to sit on. They said that they were worried that my clothes would get dirty, '*ngati sopo akudula*' (soap is expensive). Despite my initial protestations that I wanted to sit on the floor with the learners, I became accustomed to the arrangements preferred by my hosts. However, I was not comfortable, especially with the routine of going to the village headperson to borrow chairs. As a compromise, the cluster supervisor and I agreed to source at least two benches for the class.

It was thus customary that each time I went to observe the lessons, I sat on a bench which was positioned close to the southern wall next to the entrance of the classroom. The cluster supervisor and the instructors usually sat on the opposite side. The portable chalk board stood leaning against the western wall near the backroom entrance. The learners usually sat in rows on the floor facing west.

Sitting on my bench, I made 'scratch notes' which I later expanded and refined using 'headnotes' to produce 'field notes proper' (Sanjek, 1990). I also audio-recorded the lessons and transcribed the recordings not later than two days from the day the recordings were made. Apart from tape recording, I took photos of

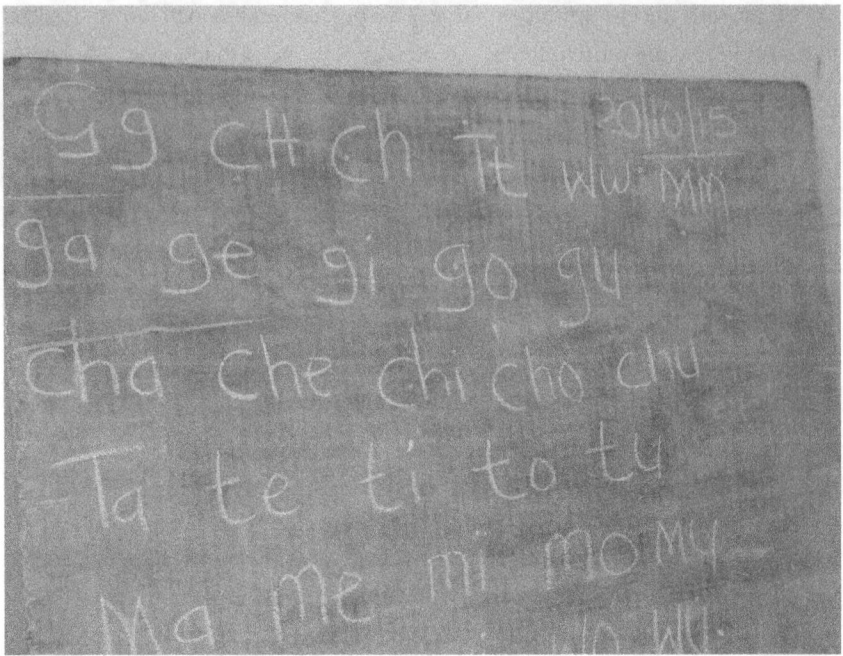

Figure 1 Chichewa Lesson

the work written on the board as shown in Figure 1 above; sometimes with the consent of the literacy learners, I took pictures of them as well as their work.

Employing participant observation in the classroom was not as easy as I had assumed. There were many things taking place at the same time in the room, causing me to ask, what is it that one should really focus upon and why? My focus wandered from the teaching and learning to relationships, as well as to what I summed up as 'school culture' (I discuss this in detail later). Participant observation was also used in other settings. The technique was employed to observe some community members such as Ms[1] Awali in their homes.

Ms Awali was a widow. She was one of the learners who were considered to be very old. She had been attending the literacy lessons since the centre was established in 2013. Apart from farming, she conducted some small-scale businesses. She brewed and sold local beer; she also sold tobacco. She was a member of one of the community savings groups, in which she was elected as a treasurer. In addition, she knitted various items on order.

---

[1] I am using this for two reasons. First, to show their gender having used surnames since in some instances the use of first names mark lack of respect in Malawi. Second, this title somehow does not show marital status.

Sitting outside my rented house (more on this later in this chapter), I observed Ms Awali conduct her businesses. In this setting, I relied heavily on taking down notes which I used to ask Ms Awali informally to clarify some of the things I saw. Sometimes we sat on a mat together and I observed her knit scarves while telling me stories about her knitting. Unlike the participant observations I had in the classroom, at home it was spontaneous: I just saw things as they came and noted down what I thought was interesting to me or needed further understanding.

Participant observation was also used to understand some tasks the women did in groups. Instead of asking them how they conducted these tasks, I participated and observed them in action. In these cases, I was not just interested in appreciating how they conducted their activities, but I was also interested in observing how the women who were taking part in the adult literacy class positioned themselves in such activities. Participating and observing in a community savings group, for instance, allowed me to see the extent to which the literacy learners were involved in this activity which required reading and writing. I bought some 'shares' in the community savings group and distributed them among all the members.

During my fieldwork, I was privileged to attend a training session for English literacy instructors. At this function, I also used participant observation to understand how such activities were carried out. This allowed me to have first-hand experience of the exercise. I interacted with both the trainers and the trainees, and I asked them what they thought about the whole exercise. I took part in the exercises the trainers had organized. However, I noted that initially the officers did not know how to treat me until I asked them to allow me to be among the trainees. I told them that I had not attended a training of that nature before. I also told them that I had gone there to learn. Notwithstanding this and the fact that all the officers knew the purpose of my participation, they still saw me as a university lecturer. For instance, during an informal conversation with two community members, Ms Naliswe and Ms Matiki, the former asked me to find a literacy centre for her to facilitate.

Researcher: No, I can't. I am not an adult literacy officer. Perhaps you can talk with the cluster supervisor. I am just someone who is observing what the people in this community do.

Ms Naliswe: No, how can you be a nobody and work at Chancellor College. You are an officer. You are a big boss.

(Field notes: 20 February 2016)

Sometimes as I observed the literacy lessons or interacted with the community members, I heard or saw things which required a direct and detailed discussion. To achieve this, I organized and conducted individual semi-structured interviews. At the beginning, I planned to hold these interviews with a few individuals who could be identified based on the issue I wanted to understand. However, once I began conducting the interviews, all the learners wanted me to visit their homes and interview them. I agreed to this as a matter of courtesy. To facilitate a smooth discussion during these interviews, I employed interview guides drawn from the issues emerging from the observational data, 'so that the content focuses on the crucial issues of the study' (Burns, 2000: 424).

I occasionally encountered a conflict of agendas. As a researcher, I had a list of issues I wanted to understand further but sometimes some of my interviewees had issues they wanted someone to listen to. This was evident from the responses they gave to some of the questions I asked. I learnt to listen to and appreciate their stories first before addressing my agenda. In this regard, these encounters were not just about data collection but they were also spaces that allowed my participants to express some of the frustrations and pains they experienced in their day-to-day lives. What concerned me most was that, despite opening up and sharing their frustrations with me, I could not do anything to help them: most of the issues they raised revolved around the politics of their community like the one involving Ms Balala cited in Chapter 4, and I did not want to ruin my relationships with the local leaders, thereby putting my research into jeopardy. Besides, I made a commitment not to put the lives of my respondents at risk. Drawing myself into those politics where others had failed would not guarantee amicable resolutions.

Apart from semi-structured interviews, most of the data I got from the cluster supervisor were collected through informal interviews (conversations). These conversations just started as any other talk, but whenever he said something that caught my attention, I followed it up by asking him specific questions. I did not write anything immediately. When I went back to my rented house or my residence, I jotted down as much as I could remember. I also used the same technique with some of the literacy learners. For instance, in most cases, I was the first person to arrive at the class. Whichever learner arrived first got involved in a conversation with me. I listened to what they said and probed for more on any issues that seemed to be of interest to me. When we got into the classroom, my first task was to jot down key points that emerged during the conversation I had just had with the learner outside while the instructors were getting prepared for the lessons to start.

Although informal interviews proved to be very useful to me, I found them difficult at the beginning, because I had an assumption that, as a researcher, I was supposed to take the lead in the data collection process. I felt that the informal interview technique did not give me a firm enough control over the proceedings. But the more I used the technique, the more conversant I became with it. I learnt to be a listener with a purpose.

In some cases, the issues I sought to explore were multifaceted and therefore required multiple perspectives from a number of people. I therefore organized and conducted FGDs. The participants who took part in these discussions shared at least one characteristic, because I was mindful that 'the rule for selecting focus group participants is commonality, not diversity' (Krueger, 1994: 14). Hence, I had FGDs with young men who were out of school, some non-literate women who were not attending literacy classes, some young women who were attending literacy lessons and some middle-aged women who were attending literacy lessons. The number of participants in the discussions ranged from two to four. The topics that were discussed ranged from their life experiences in the village, their aspirations, their perceptions of literacy in general and of adult literacy classes in particular, their experiences with literacy in some of their lived worlds, their experiences and expectations of the literacy lessons, as well as their views regarding literacy examinations.

FGDs are often criticized because it is alleged that their results may 'prove nothing, not least because the number of informants is usually small and group dynamics can mean that dominant individuals can obliterate alternative points of view' (Knight, 2002: 70). On the contrary, I found them useful because they helped me gain some insights into my participants' attitudes, feelings, perceptions and opinions towards literacy in their lived worlds. My purpose for conducting the FGDs was not to build group consensus but rather 'to promote self-disclosure among participants' (Krueger, 1994: 11). Thus, by having a couple of participants responding to the same questions in one session, I was able to get varied perspectives on the topics I sought to understand.

One of the key principles underpinning Holland *et al*'s (1998) theory of self and identity, particularly the concept of figured world, which was the lynchpin of my study, is the notion of artefacts. Holland *et al* (ibid) posit that 'artefacts are the means by which figured worlds are evoked, collectively developed, individually learned, and made socially and personally powerful' (p. 61). To have a better understanding of the lived experiences of any group of people requires paying attention to the artefacts they employ in various figured worlds. In other words, 'there is nothing to be gained, and much to be lost, by representing ... a culture as if it were an essentially oral tradition' (Hammersley & Atkinson, 2007: 133). Therefore, part of my data collection techniques involved gathering and documenting community members' artefacts. My aim was to appreciate the role these artefacts played in my participants' evolving figured worlds.

But for a number of reasons, not all the artefacts that were made available to me could be physically collected. Some of them were treasured by their owners, some were official documents that were supposed to be submitted to higher offices, while others were permanently fixed. Further, it would have been cumbersome for me to carry all those items to the UK. To deal with these challenges, I decided to photograph some of them upon getting consent from the owners. However, in some contexts, I realized that taking a photo of the artefacts excluding the people involved did not make sense; the pictures lacked the context and were therefore difficult to understand. Besides, sometimes when I asked people to have their items photographed, they asked me to photograph them as well. This raised an ethical dilemma and I had to seek further ethical clearance from my university.

Locating the research site

My study was conducted in Sawabu village which had eighty-three households and a total population of 306 residents. It is bounded by Namyaka village to the west, Makoloje to the north, Umali to the north east, Mpulula to the East, Cilanga to the south west and Cikoja village to south marked by a river called Kasupe. The village is located about 10 km away from Zomba city and about 400 metres from Malekano trading centre (see Chapter 4).

The village lies on a plain land and during the dry season the area is almost bare. Vegetation cover is almost absent except for a few patches of mango, blue gum, acacias and some few shrubs of natural trees and bamboos around clusters of houses. A few natural trees are also found around the village headperson's house and in the graveyard. The dwindling numbers of the trees were caused primarily by gardening as well as the need for fuelwood used for burning bricks and the latter was the main source of income for most young men in this village.

Travelling by public transport, especially minibuses, took one to a place called Makwale but big buses did not recognize this place as a bus stop. From Makwale, one headed eastward past a grass-thatched shelter to the south where a bicycle repairer plied his trade. The shelter had just a grass-thatched roof suspended on nine wooden poles.

Figure 2 Cluster of Houses for the Weca Family

Most of the houses in Sawabu village are clustered based on family membership. For instance, a cluster of houses belonging to the Weca family, seen in Figure 2 above, lay downslope towards Kasupe River to the south.

Historical perspectives of Sawabu village

The actual dates regarding when Sawabu village was established were difficult to ascertain. The village headperson claimed that the village was established in 1964 whereas some accounts put its establishment in the early 1990s. The latter accounts said that the village was formed in order to have a bigger share of beneficiaries from cash transfer, food relief and other related government and donor programmes. The village headperson also gave the same reason. The thinking was that, splitting large villages into several smaller ones helped in increasing the overall number of beneficiaries from government and donor agency programmes. This was the case because each village was considered and guaranteed a certain number of beneficiaries in its own right and community members discovered that when the allocations given to each of the smaller villages were added up, the total number of beneficiaries surpassed the allocation they would have received had the village not been divided up. In recent years, many villages have been formed in Malawi in this manner. The number of residents in a village varies but 'typical villages usually have 100 to 2000 people' (Chinsinga, 2006: 258).

It is worth noting that in Malawi, there are about six hierarchies of traditional leaders. The higher the hierarchy, the larger the area and power they have. At the top of the hierarchy are paramount chiefs followed by senior chiefs. Below the senior chiefs come chiefs, sub chiefs and group village headpersons, in that order. At the bottom of the ladder lie the village headpersons. Most traditional leaders in Malawi assume their position based on lineage and they receive monthly honoraria from the government commensurate with their rank.

Traditional leadership is much stronger in rural areas than it is in towns and cities mostly because in rural areas, the leaders' areas of influence are 'occupied by a largely homogenous people sharing more or less a common culture, social values and aspirations' (ibid). While the jurisdiction of traditional leaders from the rank of village headperson to senior chief is marked by both tribal and spatial boundaries, that of paramount chief is largely based on tribes. For instance, all the Yawos regardless of where they are found in Malawi, are under one paramount chief. Similarly, all the Chewas who are predominantly found in Malawi, Mozambique and Zambia have one paramount chief whose headquarters is in Zambia.

Traditional leaders have a significant role in the delivery of the NALP in Malawi. Although their major role is to adjudicate between disputes in their areas, they also act as gatekeepers to any development programme to be carried out in their areas. This is why they, especially village headpersons, sometimes have a say in the establishment of literacy classes in their areas.

The people of Sawabu village

Sawabu village is largely populated by Yawos[2] and most of them speak Ciyawo although the village headperson claimed that they were Mang'anjas. On several occasions, the women told the instructors in class that they were experiencing some difficulties in pronouncing some words in Chichewa because they were Yawos. Besides, when the village headperson introduced me to the people at one of the community meetings I attended, he told them that I was a Yawo just like them. Also, the customs and traditions the people of this village conducted

---

[2] Malawi has several tribal groups and Yawo and Mang'anja are the names of two of them. The language spoken by the Yawos is called Ciyawo and the one spoken by the Mang'anja is known as Cimang'anja.

such as the initiation of both boys and girls were in keeping with those of the Yawos I knew. In fact, a week before the end of fieldwork, the women asked for the suspension of the literacy classes to allow them to deal with the initiations of their children.

The Yawos are mostly matrilineal (see Berge, Kambewa, Munthali & Wiig, 2014). In terms of religion, most of the residents of Sawabu village were Muslims. These factors made it easy for me to work among them because apart from being Yawo I was a Muslim too. However, it was not just the religious and cultural similarities that helped me settle down easily among these people, rather it was the community members' hospitality that played a major part. In fact, although the majority of the community members identified themselves as Yawos and Muslims, the village had members of other tribes and denominations as well. There were some, such as the cluster supervisor, who were both Mang'anjas and Christians. Regardless of tribe or religion, whenever I had an opportunity to visit some community members' homes, their hospitality was the same.

Introducing Sawabu literacy classroom

Unlike the literacy classes I knew from my previous encounters which were conducted under trees or open shelters, Sawabu classes were taking place in a well-constructed, beautiful and permanent building, as shown in Figure 3. The building was situated towards the north eastern part of the village, close to the boundary with Ndembe village. It stood alone and was located about 15 metres northwest of the village headperson's house. It was initially constructed as a nursery school following a request from the village headperson to the then Member of Parliament (MP) for the area who was known for her charitable initiatives. The MP asked the community members to mould bricks and mobilize other locally available building materials. She provided cement, metal window frames, window panes, doors and metal door frames, roofing and other materials which the villagers could not afford, including paying the builders and carpenters. The nursery school occasionally operated in the morning from 8 o'clock to 11 a.m. and the adult literacy lessons were held on Mondays to Wednesdays from 2 o'clock to 4 p.m.

The room was completely empty; there was no chair or mat to sit on. The walls had nothing hanging for the adult literacy learners and the nursery school children to see or read. The room appeared somehow neglected with some litter piling up in a couple of potholes and the literacy learners often complained

Figure 3 Sawabu Literacy Class

about the floor being too dirty. It was the village headperson who was keen on ensuring that the building was secure and well maintained. Occasionally, when the floor became too dusty to sit on, the literacy learners volunteered to sweep.

The literacy classes at Sawabu village started in 2013 again at the request of the village headperson. For a village to obtain a literacy centre in Malawi, there are different ways that can be followed. A traditional leader can ask the relevant authorities to establish such classes in their community. Secondly, a group of community members can demand for the introduction of the classes. Or thirdly, literacy officers from the government or NGO can approach and ask the village headpersons if they would like such classes in their village. When a community agrees to have such a class, it selects a committee to oversee its operation. At Sawabu literacy centre such a committee was elected by the learners during my fieldwork in 2015.

Since 2013, only Chichewa literacy lessons were being taught at the centre. English literacy classes officially began in March 2016. The English literacy lessons were being held in the backroom, whereas the main room hosted the Chichewa literacy classes. Two instructors facilitated the lessons. Neither one facilitated the lessons on behalf of the other when the responsible instructor was absent. Apart from the two instructors, the cluster supervisor who resided in this village almost always came to the classes and in most cases stood in for the Chichewa instructor whenever she was absent. He rarely facilitated English literacy lessons, arguing that he was never trained to handle such classes. Occasionally, an instructor from a nearby dysfunctional centre also helped in facilitating the Chichewa lessons at this centre.

The research site: Dilemmas and opportunities

When I was preparing for my fieldwork, I identified a number of activities I would participate in and observe within my research site, such as Chichewa and English literacy classes, social, public and traditional events, cooperative and business groups, sanitation and nutrition activities, home and work-related activities. So, when on 24 October 2015, the supervisor took me around, showing me the village boundaries, I had these in mind. However, our preliminary informal conversations during this tour revealed that many of the activities I had outlined in my plan were non-existent in this village. This realization somehow deflated my enthusiasm. I was not sure that this was the *ideal* community for my research. In my view, the village lacked most of things I thought were crucial both for my study and for my day-to-day wellbeing.

For instance, the village had no established playground, shop or market. Instead, some community members had benches on which they sold items such as tomatoes, dried fish, onions and charcoal. Others sold salt, matches and some small confectionaries either from their benches or through the windows of their homes. The nearest recognizable shops and a market were at Malekano, seen in Figure 4, about some 400 metres away from the village centre. These shops stocked only basic items, so that if one wanted to buy any essential items of good quality, one had to go to Zomba city. To play or watch some games such as football, one had to go to Tupoce trading centre about 1½ km away. What this meant was that socializing with some of the community members who were not taking part in any group-organized activities was going to be rather very difficult.

The village did not have electricity. Only one house had a solar panel on the roof. Phone charging and other activities that required electricity were done at Malekano. The phones were charged either in shops or video showrooms but one had to pay. Most of the messages the instructors sent were delivered by word of mouth.

Figure 4 Malekano Trading Centre

The village had no mosque or church; one had to look for these services elsewhere. Community members from this village went to Mpulula, Malekano and Cikoja to pray if they were Muslims. The only nearby church I saw belonged to the Baptists and it was located in Namyaka village about 500 metres away from Sawabu literacy class.

Moreover, no formal school was located in this village. The children who were doing their primary school went to Naula, Akapela, Cipago and Alukosyo. But these schools were difficult to reach. The children had to cross the main road to go to Akapela and Alukosyo primary schools. To go to Cipago primary school, they had to cross Kasupe River using an unsafe temporary wooden bridge as shown in the picture that follows. In both cases, it was dangerous for young children.

Although statistics for the village were not available, it appeared that many children were withdrawing from school before completing primary level.

Figure 5 Wooden Bridge to Cipago across Kasupe River

The village headperson lamented this problem during a general meeting with his subjects at his compound. Sitting outside my rented house, I saw some children of school-going age just loitering around during school hours. Some of them spent most of their time watching films in video showrooms at Malekano.

The only thing I could see in this community which was also in my plan was the adult literacy class. For someone who by the end of the study was expected to write a thesis good enough for the award of a PhD, this state of affairs was more than demoralizing. However, with time I slowly began to understand the lives of the people of Sawabu village. I realized that communities are not discrete and autonomous entities; rather they are interdependent. And it became clear to me that village settings were more complex than I thought.

I saw cases where houses were physically located in one village but the occupants who were bona fide members of the village gave allegiances to another village. I was told that such allegiances were common in many places and that they were instigated by what the community members considered to be their village headpersons' favouritism when choosing beneficiaries of various government and NGO aid programmes. Feeling sidelined by their leaders, they therefore switched their allegiances to and registered their names with the village

Figure 6 Video Showroom at Malekano

headpersons they thought would consider them in such programmes. Despite making such changes, they continued to live in the village of the headperson they had broken ties with. There were also instances where plots of land were physically located within the borders of one village but it was claimed that they belonged to another village. What this meant was that drawing maps for such villages could be a very complex task. These complexities made me rethink my conceptualization of 'community'. I realized that my participants were brought together not just by the commonalities of the places they lived in, but also by some other underlying currents.

In the end, although the absence of many things limited my space for socializing with some community members in the village, there were some activities taking place in the community which were not in my initial plan. Three of these were community savings groups, cash transfer and emergency food aid programmes. Being literacy-mediated social activities that defined part of the community members' daily lives, these activities were equally important.

The village also had a nursery school, although its operation was rather erratic; the cause of this was rather difficult to establish. The caregivers of the nursery school put the blame on the parents' lack of interest, while the parents blamed it on the caregivers' lack of dedication to their work. In addition, the village had water taps planted at each cluster of houses belonging to major families. Members surrounding and using each tap were required to contribute K150.00 (less than a penny) per month. The money realized was used to pay for the bill each tap incurred which was a flat rate of K1500.00 (just over £1) per month.

Other sources of water were a borehole and a well. While the borehole was not functional because it required some repairs, the well appeared to have been neglected, left gaping dangerously in the bushes along the Sawabu and Mpulula boundary; it was mostly used by brick makers. In terms of health facilities, Sawabu and the surrounding villages were served by a government clinic which was in group village headperson Mpale's area across Kasupe River (see Figure 7).

While as a stranger I was bothered about the absence of some facilities and activities within the confines of this village, community members appeared to have been used to the situation. To them, ownership of facilities or activities cut across village boundaries. In any case, Sawabu village was a part of a broader traditional and cultural set-up; hence it had strong traditional and historical linkages with the surrounding communities. This state of affairs made me realize that ethnographic research is not about ticking the boxes in your plan but rather about exploring and understanding the complexities of the community members' lived experiences through their own lenses.

Figure 7 Tupoce Clinic

Research and context: Ethical dilemmas

Any study that involves human beings is required to provide a detailed account on how to handle ethical issues. Although this process is considered to be a standard practice, the challenge is that the yardstick used to determine ethical compliance is generally not contextualized. This is the case because the demands made, generally based on the procedures rooted in the global North, are assumed to be 'culturally neutral' and therefore universally applicable. My own experience suggests otherwise. I followed the assumed standard procedure of explaining the nature and purpose of my research to both the instructors and the adult literacy learners. I informed them that I would be meeting each one of them separately so as to get their individual consent and sign the consent forms. All of them said that they did not see any need for signing such forms. They said that they were all happy to have me as their visitor in their community. They told me that they were used to having visitors like me. To avoid arousing unnecessary suspicion, I settled for oral consent.

Kachiwanda (2009) explains similar ethical dilemmas in her study conducted in another part of Malawi. Shamim and Qureshi (2013) discuss the same ethical challenges, arguing that, although informed consent as a 'written document' is regarded as the norm, 'in some cultures, like Pakistan, oral or informal consent is more binding on the participants than formal written consent' (p. 472). They observe that in their context, 'a written consent form is regarded with suspicion, especially in non-literate communities' (ibid).

For me, getting written consent, let alone informed consent, proved to be very problematic in some contexts. For instance, sometimes I attended community meetings as well as funerals. On such occasions, while the village headman and his counsellors[3] knew who I was and what I was doing, some of the people present did not. In these circumstances, it was practically impossible and culturally inappropriate to go around asking people to sign informed consent forms.

Sometimes new adult learners joined the literacy classes while the lessons were in progress. In such circumstances, I could not tell the instructor to stop the lessons to allow me get informed consent from such learners. The best I could do was to ask for such consent retrospectively. What this means is that

---

[3] These are members of the village whom traditional leaders identify mostly from major families to act as their confidants, advisors and the jury during case hearings.

I used my own judgement as to when it was feasible and ideal for me to seek informed consent and in all such cases I got it orally.

Part of my data collection techniques involved photography. When I was applying for ethical clearance, I indicated that I was going to take pictures of artefacts only. However, due to the circumstances I discussed earlier, I ended up asking for additional ethical clearance from my university to allow me to take pictures of people as well. Accordingly, I sought consent from the community members I photographed to use some of their photos in my thesis. However, because of the 'non-tangibility of oral consent and the difficulty of documenting it for the public gaze' (Shamim & Qureshi, 2013: 473), I was not able to use those photos in my work. Somehow, I felt a sense of betrayal. I imagined the disappointment community members may have upon realizing that none of their pictures would be used as agreed. Perhaps this is an example of a situation in which 'existing ethical codes and paradigms' tend 'to be rather restrictive and insensitive to multiple and complex cultural and contextual differences' (Robinson-Pant & Singal, 2013: 417).

The ethnographer: A stranger with many faces

A researcher who employs an ethnographic approach inevitably cultivates close relationships with the community members in her or his quest to become part of the community. In my case, such relationships imposed some 'responsibilities' on me which in turn triggered 'issues of obligation, reciprocity and trust' (Madden, 2010: 16). As such, my fieldwork was not just about collecting data for my study but also about playing my role as a responsible member of the community.

The ethnographer as a resource person

The adult literacy primer does not just deal with matters of reading and writing. It also covers knowledge on a wide range of fields. Having knowledge in all these fields sometimes posed a challenge to the literacy instructors. Occasionally, they faced situations whereby they did not have adequate knowledge concerning the issues their lesson was dealing with. When this happened, they often asked me to help. Although sometimes I protested and informed them that I did not have the expertise, I usually obliged and helped them with the little I knew. Being a teacher myself, I sympathized and understood the awkward positions they were in. I helped in explaining issues in areas such as health, natural resources, gender and sexuality, language, civic education and arithmetic. Thus, despite my limitations in other fields, I became an expert in almost everything. This state of affairs made me wonder as to how these instructors coped with such situations every year. On paper, the NALP expects officers from other Ministries and non-governmental organizations to help the instructors explain the subject matter that require expert knowledge (see Ministry of Women and Child Welfare and Community Services, n.d.; Rokadiya, 1986). However, during my entire fieldwork period, I saw none.

The ethnographer as a co-instructor

Apart from helping the literacy instructors in explaining certain issues during the lessons, I was sometimes involved in the actual facilitation. In the Chichewa literacy classroom, the instructors occasionally asked me to mark the learners' work. In some cases, I found that the learners had not understood what was taught. I therefore sat down with the learners and explained to them what the lesson was all about. Also, when the English classes began, I was occasionally given the class to facilitate. This happened mostly when the instructor was absent. Generally, the learners who were in the English class did not want to be combined with the Chichewa learners and do Chichewa lessons. They wanted to learn English. At the same time, the supervisor did not want to send the learners home when their instructor was absent. He said that he was afraid that if he did so, they might lose interest and eventually decide to withdraw from the classes. In such circumstances, I was asked to deal with the English lesson, since he argued that he was not trained to handle such lessons.

Generally, I found this change in roles to be both rewarding and challenging. It was rewarding in the sense that I viewed it as a form of giving back to the community. Besides, it gave me the opportunity to experience and appreciate how it was to facilitate in an adult literacy class. However, despite my teaching experience, I found it very difficult, because I needed to balance between helping the literacy learners on the one hand, and collecting the data I needed for my thesis on the other. Besides, I had my own assumptions and beliefs regarding literacy in general, and teaching adult learners in particular. Trying to ignore my assumptions and beliefs and doing the work as it was required by the literacy providers was not an easy thing to do.

The ethnographer as a benefactor

My participation in the adult literacy class helped me question some of my assumptions and have a second thought about certain things I took for granted. Watching the learners do the work in class, I noted that some learners wrote their work on pieces of paper. I wondered whether they would be able to keep such papers for future reference. I asked the instructors why this was the case and they told me that those learners did not have notebooks. The issue here was not that they could not afford to buy one but rather, given the little they had, their priority lay on using it to take care of their families. I felt sorry for them and sourced some notebooks and pens which were distributed among all the learners. But I soon realized that this gesture reinforced my identity as a Malawi government employee as well as a university teacher. The gesture elevated my status in the village. I was now seen as someone who did not lack financial resources. Before long, the learners asked me to provide them with pieces of cloth which they said they wanted to put on as uniform for the school. Reluctantly, I granted them what they requested. My worry was that these acts would turn the school into a site for charity. I shared these fears with the supervisor. Although he agreed with my observations, he told me that the practice was not new, since the government used to provide the literacy learners with such pieces of cloth, especially when there was an official function.

My fears were confirmed when a few weeks before the end of my fieldwork, the adult learners asked me to provide them with another set of cloth for the same purpose, arguing that since I was leaving, I was supposed to give them something to remember me. This time, I jokingly reasoned with them that 'culturally' when someone is leaving, it is the responsibility of those remaining behind to give something to the one leaving and not the other way round. I informed them that I was worried that buying them another set of pieces of cloth may send a wrong signal about the school. They all seemed to agree with me. They even noted that some individuals just came to receive the pieces of cloth I bought the previous year and never came back. We therefore decided to organize a good-bye and farewell function instead, whereby we had some drinks, plays, songs, poems and group photos. We also exchanged gifts. I used the opportunity both to thank them for sharing with me their life experiences and to encourage them to continue with their literacy lessons.

Generally, employing participant observation in an adult literacy classroom made me realize that an adult literacy classroom is very complex and therefore needed far more than just being 'there' in order to understand it. It provided me with a unique experience. I was amazed by how each day the classroom appeared to have different 'characters'. Adult literacy learners frequently changed their statuses. For instance, at one moment a learner would say that they were not able to read, only to see them volunteer themselves to read a paragraph moments later. The converse was also true. In this regard, one needed to have a third eye, so as to capture the nuances of the classroom interaction.

Conclusion

Generally, the issue of which approach to employ in a study depends on a number of factors such as the research question and objectives as well as the researcher's ontological and epistemological orientations. My study was about understanding some community members' literacy practices, discourses, meanings, identities and power relationships in some of their lived worlds. To unpack these issues, I chose to employ an ethnographic approach because I believed that to understand them better, I needed to live and interact with the community members more closely. However, a researcher employing this approach is required to be mindful about the illusion that living among the research participants automatically translates into becoming a 'full' member of the community. My experience shows that the social status one already acquired stands out more than the one she or he attempts to cultivate. During my entire fieldwork, I tried all I could to dress, eat and do the things the community members did. But as I have noted in this chapter, the community members knew who I was and accorded me the same position I was trying hard to downplay. I was amazed when Ms Matiki, one of the literacy learners, said to me during an informal conversation, '*When you walk together with the instructors, even a child would know that you are more educated than them.*'

This chapter has highlighted how the research site sometimes shapes the way an ethnographic researcher conducts his or her study. Just as I tried not to put the lives of my participants at risk, I also applied the same measures towards my safety and this had some implication on what I was able to personally experience in the community.

Realizing that it would be 'inhumane and deeply disrespectful' (Cohen *et al*, 2007: 60) to stay in a community for a long time, developing friendships in the process, and then just leave without giving back to the people, I attempted to provide 'some form of reciprocity as a small reward for [my] participants' (Creswell, 2014: 254). Such reciprocity in some cases means playing different roles which might reinforce the way the community members perceive the researcher.

The dilemmas of implementing ethical principles grounded within the perspectives, norms and practices prevalent in global North perhaps mirror 'the need to reflect on ethics in the context of morality and to start from an acknowledgement of likely differences, rather than the assumption of universally shared ethical principles and practices' (Robinson-Pant & Singal, 2013: 459).

Overall, my ethnographic experience made me realize that the fundamental lessons one learns from an ethnographic study may not be fully captured in the narrative produced after the study, because such lessons are written in one's soul.

4

Literacy Practices in Community Members' Lived Worlds

The hallmark of the social theory of literacy is the postulation that literacy is not one and the same thing in all contexts; rather it varies. Hence proponents of this theory find it useful to talk about multiple literacies to capture this situated nature of literacy (see Chapter 2). In this regard, what may not be considered to be literacy in one context sometimes gains currency and becomes a major kind of literacy in another. As I noted in Chapter 3, one of my data collection techniques involved gathering artefacts. In this chapter, I discuss community members' literacy practices and artefacts in some organized and identifiable literacy-mediated social activities which I frame as figured worlds (refer to Chapter 2). Specifically, my account focuses on government- and donor-assisted initiatives, particularly the Joint Emergency Food Assistance Programme, the Malawi Social Cash Transfer Programme and the Farm Input Subsidy Programme. The focus is to map out the literacy practices and artefacts the community members encountered in their lived worlds with a view to underscoring the contextual nature of literacy. The discussion raises a key question as to whether the one-size-fits-all approach to literacy teaching and learning that was taking place at the Sawabu literacy centre would address the literacy needs of the people in the village.

My fieldwork took place at a time when many parts of Malawi, including my research site, were experiencing acute food shortages. This situation had arisen because in part, during the previous growing season, the country had received more rain than required, thereby affecting food crop production. Apart from affecting crop yields, the heavy rains made some community members homeless. To alleviate the problems people were facing, there were some food relief programmes being carried out in many parts of Malawi including my research site.

The emergency food assistance programme

One of the initiatives that helped communities to obtain some relief food was run jointly by the Malawi government and the World Food Programme (WFP). This initiative was part of what the WFP called Protracted Relief and Recovery Operation (PRRO). The aim of this initiative was 'to contribute to restoring food security, rebuilding sustainable livelihoods and strengthening the resilience of the most vulnerable food-insecure population' (WFP, 2016: n.p.). Thus, through the PRRO, WFP provided relief assistance to people affected by disasters. In Malawi's case, the initiative sought to provide 'emergency food assistance to food-insecure people affected by shocks …' (ibid).

In the aim cited above, WFP spelled out the purpose, nature and possible beneficiaries of its initiative. It presented a figured world populated by people who had been struck by natural disasters. It constructed the victims of such disasters as 'food-insecure', a condition which guaranteed them legitimacy as actors in the figured world of emergency food assistance programme. What this suggested was that any member of the community whose food-insecurity did not arise from the effects of the officially recognized disaster was denied access to this figured world. In other words, the word 'emergency' related more to disaster than it did to food-insecurity. Such figuring had some implications in the way community members perceived the programme, especially considering the fact that despite their houses not collapsing, some of them had lost their livelihoods owing to the same heavy rains.

In the vernacular language, the emergency food assistance programme was called '*zogwa manyumba*' (about/of collapsed houses), because initially it targeted only those community members whose houses had collapsed as a result of the heavy rains. It was understood that anyone whose house had collapsed, but had immediately decided to reconstruct it, was ruled out as a potential actor in this figured world. As a result, one year after the said disaster, I saw houses of some of the beneficiaries still standing with one or two walls demolished. No attempt was made to rebuild them, apparently to legitimize their continued participation in this figured world. That is, they identified themselves as individuals who needed support, and their partially collapsed houses became one of the key artefacts that evoked their figured world of the emergency food assistance programme. All community members who were identified and recruited into this programme were given a ration card (see Figure 8).

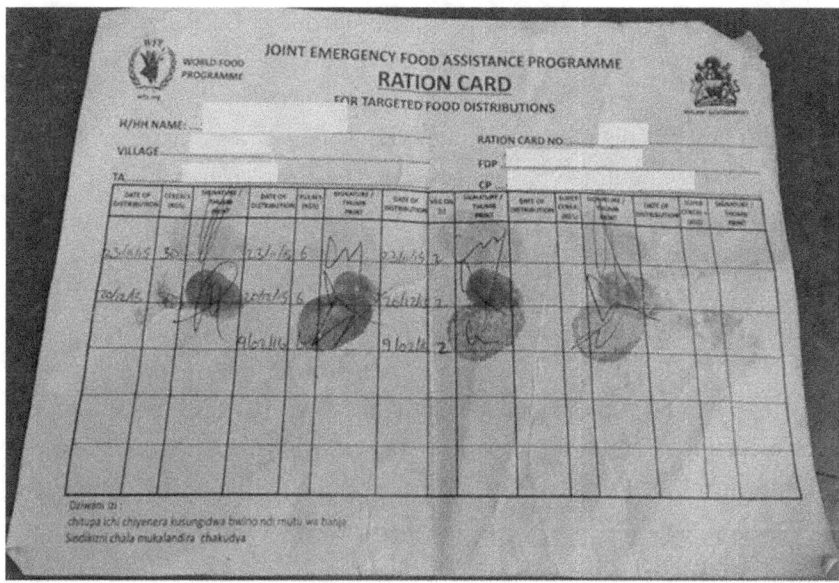

Figure 8 Ration Card

The card was divided up into columns. Each item to be distributed had its own column, that is, cereals, pulses and vegetable oil. The other columns were for dates and signatures or thumb printing. Apparently, these details were aimed at promoting transparency and accountability, and the logos at the top end of the card gave it its authority and authenticity. What this suggested was that the literacy practices and the artefact employed in this figured world required the actors to have knowledge not only of how to read and enumerate but also of the values the artefact sought to promote. Besides, participants were required to have knowledge of measures of weight and volume to ascertain that the amounts they received were correct. Here too it meant that a single de-contextualized literacy was not enough for the community members to navigate through this figured world.

The situation was compounded by the choice of language(s). The card employed two languages, namely English and Chichewa. By choosing the two languages in a multilingual country like Malawi, the producers of this document assumed that the beneficiaries of the programme would be able to understand them. However, my experience in other contexts suggests that this assumption was rather questionable. At the same time, by using two languages in the way they did, the producers of the card exercised power in deciding which information should be relatively accessible to the community members. Thus, all relevant parts of the card were written in English which suggested that the intended audience were officers of the programme. Chichewa was used to provide instructions on who should keep the card and what the beneficiaries should do when they receive their rations.

A closer look at the ration card suggested that it was serving more than one purpose. For the community members, it identified them as legitimate beneficiaries of the programme. As such, it did not just provide its holder access to this world, but also ascribed them an identity of being a victim of 'shocks' and therefore, 'food-insecure'. For the Malawi government and the World Food Programme, the card facilitated their bureaucratic practices, that is, office record keeping.

Whereas the food aid programme was necessitated by torrential rains which swept away people's crops and damaged their homes, food insecurity is a perennial issue in Malawi in general and at Sawabu village in particular. This is why some of the stories in the NALP primer are on farming with an aim of helping rural people to accept 'innovations and modernisation'.

'Modern' farming

The Ministry of Women and Children Affairs and Community Services (n.d.) states that one of the objectives of the National Adult Literacy Programme is, in part, 'to assist in achieving government development objectives by enabling rural populations to take advantage of modern and effective farming techniques to increase their overall productivity' (p. 3). In this case, the Ministry assumes that the cause of the apparent low productivity among the rural populations is lack of knowledge of 'modern and effective farming' methods. It constructs a figured world of 'modern' farming to which it presumably wants to recruit the 'rural populations'. To disseminate the purported 'modern and effective farming techniques', Ministry of Agriculture emphasizes offering extension services to all communities in Malawi. In these initiatives, the focus is on helping community members to master what are considered to be the best agricultural practices. Part of this initiative involves the distribution of leaflets such as the one shown in Figure 9.

Many community members in Sawabu village had received and kept this agricultural leaflet. I was told that the agricultural extension worker for the area gave them the leaflet when he came to advise them on best farming practices. The purpose of this leaflet was to disseminate knowledge whose practical application would, it was assumed, lead the individual to becoming an actor in the figured world of 'modern' farming.

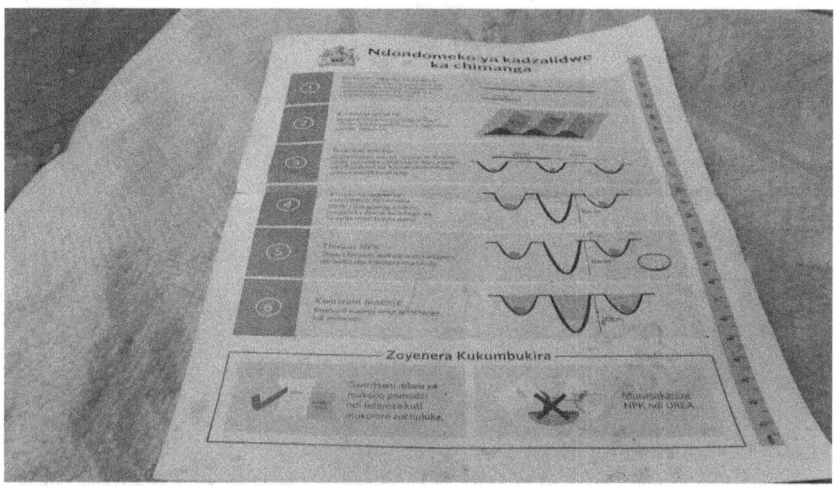

Figure 9 An Agricultural Leaflet

The leaflet provided six steps community members were supposed to follow in order to improve their agricultural productivity. It privileged certain distances between ridges and planting stations, the depth of the planting stations and the number of seeds per station. It also provided tips on how to apply fertilizers.

The leaflet instructed the farmers to have two sticks measuring 75 cm and 25 cm respectively. The 75-cm stick was to be used to determine distances between ridges while the 25-cm one would measure distances between planting stations. One seed per planting station was recommended. In this regard, its producers assumed that the users had numeracy skills and that they knew the metric system of measurements. To help the farmers measure the sticks accurately, the leaflet was calibrated in centimetres like a ruler (see the yellow strip on the right of the leaflet in Figure 9 above). Steps 1 to 3 spell out these measurements. Steps 4 to 6 are about fertilizer application. It showed that the hole in which the fertilizer should be put should be made exactly midway between the planting stations and that it should be 10-cm deep although the leaflet did not explain how the depth would be measured. It also showed the amount of fertilizer to be applied in each hole, that is, one bottle top.

Ms Awali told me that the village had a small experimental garden in which the extension worker helped them apply these techniques. However, transferring the practice to their own gardens proved problematic, especially when it came to practically measuring the distances and the depths as required by the 'modern techniques' of farming. (See Figure 10.)

Figure 10 Spacing in a Maize Garden

This picture shows that the spacing of the crops varied and in many cases each planting station had more than one seed.

One of the key features of this leaflet was that it was multimodal in many respects. First, it called for a combination of literacy and numeracy practices. In others parts, it required visual and numeracy abilities. Hence, one was supposed to have multiple competencies to understand it.

The leaflet also portrayed some information as being very important. Using lines, the leaflets highlighted some information at the bottom and enclosed it in a rectangle. This information was captioned: *What must be remembered*. Even here, the information was given using different modes. It employed school practices of using ticks and crosses. However, just like the other visuals, the ticks, crosses and the illustrations on their own could not convey the intended message fully in the absence of the written words. One was required to read the written text. Besides, one was supposed to know what ticks and crosses meant in this context.

The leaflet promoted the use of hybrid seeds together with fertilizers but disapproved of mixing NPK and UREA fertilizers. Realizing that many smallholder maize farmers could not afford to buy these farm inputs and participate in the figured world of 'modern' farming, the Malawi Government has been running a farm input subsidy programme since the 2005/2006 growing season. The programme was said to target smallholder farmers who are resource-poor but own a piece of land. The targeting criteria also recognise special vulnerable groups, such as guardians looking after physically challenged persons; child-headed, female-headed and orphan-headed households; and households affected by HIV and AIDS.

(Future Agricultures, 2013: n.p.)

The main aim of the Malawi Farm Input Subsidy Programme (FISP) is to enhance productivity with a view to attaining food security for the country. As can be deduced from the quotation above, FISP is a programme that targets some selected individuals in the communities. Once registered, the beneficiaries are given coupons towards the start of the rainy season. To receive the coupons, the registered community members are requested to convene together with members of other communities at a designated place. The responsible officers call out the names of registered beneficiaries, village by village. Any member whose name is called out goes forward to receive their coupons. Before getting their coupons, the members are asked to sign their names or print using their thumbs. Some community members resented this practice because to some extent it compelled them to reveal their literacy identity. In this regard, although thumb printing was officialized in many figured worlds in Malawi, the practice aroused mixed feeling among community members. (I discuss this later.)

In other programmes, such as the Malawi Social Cash Transfer programme, documents similar to the agricultural leaflet were used and the same assumption was made regarding their prospective readers by conveying the messages in Chichewa. Despite such efforts, the documents still demanded a great deal of reading and calculations, as discussed in the section which follows.

Social cash transfer programme

Apart from the joint emergency food assistance programme, some community members were benefiting from the Malawi Social Cash Transfer Programme which was locally known as *Mtukula Pakhomo* (which can literally be translated as 'the household developer'). According to the Food and Agriculture Organisation (FAO) of the United Nations (2014: 5), the aim of the Malawi Social Cash Transfer was

> to provide regular small amounts of cash to very poor households that were also deemed 'labour-constrained' – unable to generate sufficient income through

labour – owing to reasons such as old age, disability, chronic illness or having a very high ratio of child and elderly dependants to working-age adults.

Unlike the emergency food assistance programme, the social cash transfer was constructed as the figured world of the 'ultra-poor and labour constrained'. It was populated by individuals who were seen to be unable to work and get some income due to old age, disability, chronic illness and the assumed burden of having too many dependants. Therefore, although poverty was a necessary condition for one to become an actor in this figured world, it was not sufficient. However, recruiting actors to participate in this figured world was not easy because there were just too many people who considered themselves as the 'ultra-poor and labour constrained'. For instance, Ms Balala persistently bemoaned the fact that she was unfairly denied the opportunity to be recruited as an actor in this figured world. She told me that she was registered during the preliminary registration process and that she was given a slip that legitimized her participation (see Figure 11). She said that she was surprised that her name was missing on the final list of beneficiaries.

> *They told us to keep the slip they gave us. They said we were going to use it to receive the money once the programme started. Then we were called to be photographed. Before the names were called out, the officials had a meeting behind the court. When they came back, they said whoever hears their name is the one who is going to benefit from the programme. The names were printed from the computer. But on this day, they were deleting some names with a pen. Does a computer have a pen? No it does not! I saw it with my own eyes. They deleted my name with a pen to bar me from receiving the money.*
> (Field notes: 2 December 2015)

The significance of this slip to the community members was that it separated the holder from the other community members by projecting them as potential

Figure 11 Registration Slip

actors in the figured world of the 'ultra-poor and labour constrained'. The problem it created, however, was that it gave false hopes to households that were screened out in the process, as was the case with Ms Balala.

Like the Joint Emergency Food Assistance Programme, the Social Cash Transfer Programme was executed at community level through a committee called Community Social Support Committee (CSSC). This committee identified and assessed the potential actors to be recruited into this figured world. The beneficiary identification process took two stages involving different literacy practices. First, the CSSC members identified and assessed the potential beneficiary households. They asked the head of the identified households some questions printed on a form and their answers were recorded on the same. After this exercise, the head of the household was given a slip shown in Figure 11.

The information gathered by the CSSC was relayed to the district office and it was punched into the computer which selected the eligible persons based on the information given. Community members whose names finally appeared on the list of approved beneficiaries were given several documents, including the leaflet shown in Figure 12. The purpose of this leaflet was to make the beneficiaries understand how the programme worked. Most of it was written in Chichewa.

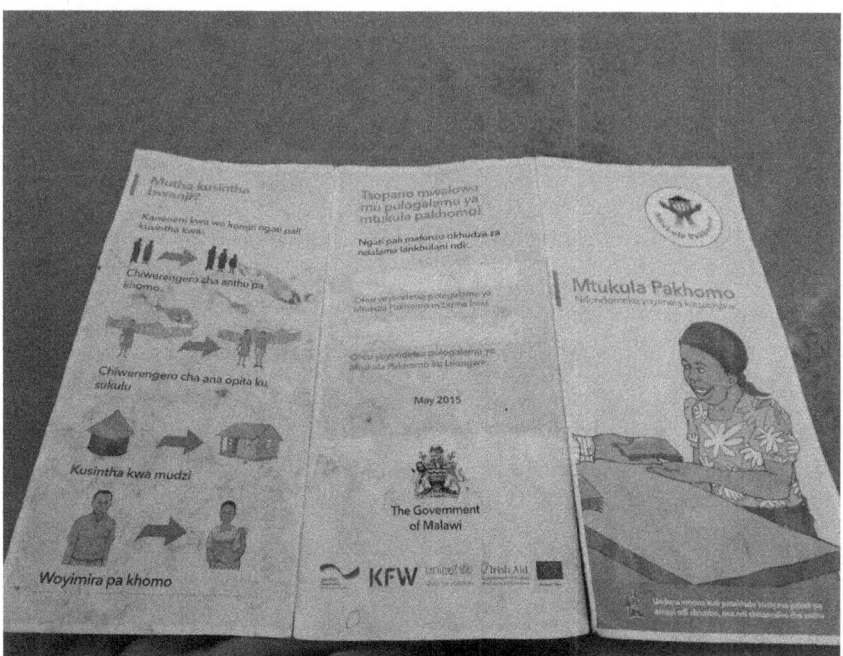

Figure 12 The Malawi Social Cash Transfer Programme Leaflet (Outer pages)

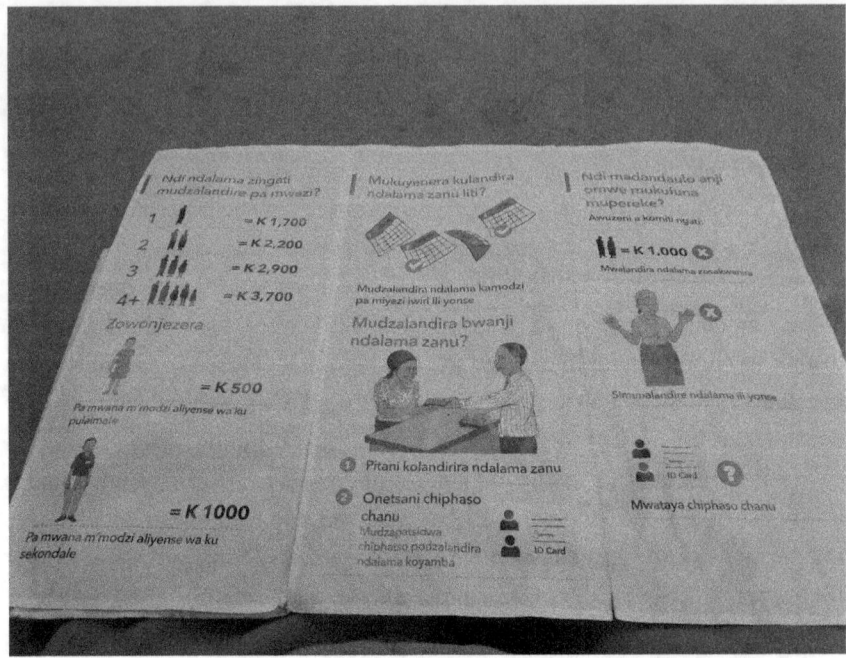

Figure 13 The Malawi Social Cash Transfer Programme Leaflet (Inner pages)

The outer pages of the leaflet informed the recipients that they were now actors in the (figured) world of Social Cash Transfer Programme. It also informed them where to go in the event that they had any queries. It explained to the beneficiaries the process to be followed in case there were some changes concerning the beneficiaries.

From right to left, the inner pages show the kind of queries the beneficiaries could launch such as receiving less money than stipulated, not receiving money at all or loss of money card.

What is important to note is that the leaflet used written words, images (visual literacy), figures and mathematical symbols to convey the information required. This meant that for one to understand this leaflet, the ability to read in Chichewa was not sufficient. For instance, on the left part of Figure 13 above, the participants were required to understand the links between the images, mathematical symbols and the figures. Besides, the leaflet was folded, hence it required additional competencies to figure out where to start from, when reading it.

The community members who were eventually registered for the programme received another artefact, the money card. Legitimate participation in this

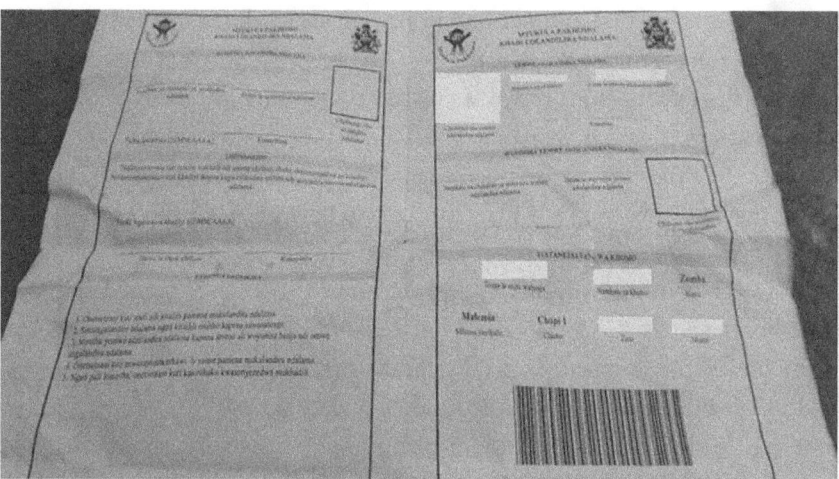

Figure 14 Beneficiary Money Card (Inner pages)

world required the production of this artefact. Each time the beneficiary went to receive the money they carried with them their card. The officers of the programme used the spaces at the back of this card to record the money that was due to the beneficiary and the latter either signed their name or printed using their thumb. Here too, the practice required the beneficiaries to reconcile the amounts written on their cards with the money they had received before appending their signatures.

Just like the food ration card, the format of money card showed that it was meant for office use. It was very detailed in terms of personal information. As Figure 14 shows, the money card required the beneficiary to affix a photograph to authenticate their identity. It also had a barcode at the bottom. It provided some space on the left page where an officer was supposed to certify both the identity of the card holder as well as its use. The discourse employed in this part was legal which could be translated as follows: *I certify that the owner of this card is the one whose photograph is affixed on it.* Generally, this was one way of assuring the donors that there was transparency and accountability in the programme.

In terms of language, the card was written mostly in Chichewa with English words being used in a few places. Ms Ulaya, the only beneficiary of the programme in the village, told me that she kept this card in a secure place *'because we were urged to take care of the document on which our photos appeared. "If you lose this one, it means that you shall not be able to receive money"'* (Field notes: 11 February 2016). The officers' advice emphasized the fact that the money card was a key artefact that allowed one to participate in the figured world of the 'ultra-poor and labour constrained'.

What these discussions reveal is that the community members encountered various artefacts which demanded varied literacies. The implication of this was that the single literacy some of them were learning at the Sawabu literacy centre may not have been adequate for them to navigate through all these social worlds. Suffice to say that most of the community members did not put much emphasis on reading the artefacts they were given. They used these documents for other purposes. For instance, when I asked Ms Awali as to whether she read and followed the instructions on the agricultural leaflet I looked at earlier, she told me that she had read just the heading and could not read the rest due to font size. She said that she just folded it and kept it in her suitcase and used it as a memento for her participation in the experimental garden. Other community members who also had this leaflet told me similar stories. The same was the case with the other artefacts such as the ration card and the money card which the beneficiaries used as identity cards. What this means was that the reading and understanding of these documents appeared not to be the primary concern of the beneficiaries. This was the case because they did not need to read them; the programme officers and some members of the Community Social Support Committee provided them the information they needed whenever possible. In some cases, they relied on other people's help to navigate through the activities which required reading and writing.

Literacy mediation

In the preceding sections, I have alluded to the fact that non-literate community members who participated in literacy-mediated activities got help from others. One such individual was Ms Duniya.

Ms Duniya was a village headperson of Makoloje village which initially was part of Sawabu village. She was an adult literacy learner who had not had any primary schooling owing to problems of fees. She told me that her husband was keen on teaching her how to read and write but she did not have a primer. As a traditional leader, she was involved in many activities that required reading and writing. To navigate through some of these activities, she needed support and she told me that

> when settling cases, I rely on my councillors, my young sister and my niece. These people write the deliberations during the cases and sometimes they ask me to pass

judgement. In terms of summons, it is my young sister and my niece who help out in writing those and I stamp them.

(Field notes: 17 January 2016)

Ms Duniya's remarks showed that, despite the literacy demands of her office and her being non-literate, she was able to carry out her duties with the help of others. That is, literacy mediation was central in discharging her leadership role in her community.

It was not just Ms Duniya who participated in literacy-mediated activities through the help of others; Ms Suya did the same. Ms Suya was the youngest of the three sisters in a family of ten children, five boys and five girls. Ms Suya as well as her siblings did not attend formal school because their parents could not afford to pay school fees. Despite her lack of formal education which resulted in her being labelled 'illiterate', Ms Suya was not attending literacy lessons because she considered herself old. She told me that she occasionally participated in activities where literacy had a role. She said that

> sometimes we conducted elections to elect group leaders. During such elections they said that we should write down names of people we wanted to get positions. They said they did not want the show of hands or lining up behind a candidate. In such situations, I made sure that I sat close to someone who knew how to read and write. I gave my paper to that person and whispered into her ears the name of my preferred candidate. Once they write for me, I cast my vote.

(Field notes: 18 June 2016)

This excerpt shows Ms Suya's inability to read and write did not stop her from participating in the elections that required such abilities and that she knew how to handle herself in such situations. In fact, she made a strong case for literacy mediation when she talked about non-literate persons boarding wrong buses, saying,

> they choose to board the wrong buses. Some of us when we travel, we make sure we link up with passengers travelling on the same route. When we get tickets, we listen carefully and when you hear someone talking about boarding the bus which we are also waiting for, we keep an eye on them. When we see them boarding the bus, we follow them. In fact, these days they always tell you where the bus is going and if one boards a wrong one, they do so by choice. Why can't they ask? Even those people who can read and write do sometimes ask, so what is the problem with that? Look, here in the village, our roads do not have sign posts. So even those people who can read and write ask for directions here and there is no problem.

(Field notes: 18 June 2016)

Although some critics may question Ms Suya's strategies and some of the examples she gave, she still made a point that literacy mediation was not a practice reserved for individuals deemed to be non-literate. In her view, even those assumed to be literate sometimes do ask about which buses were going where. In this case, Ms Suya's position challenged one of the reasons some adult literacy learners often cited for their involvement in literacy lessons. She did not see any problem in asking other people for help. In fact, she said that she used to get letters from her husband when he was still alive. She said: *When I got such letters, I found someone to read for me. I also found someone to write letters for me to respond to my husband's letters. Everything went on smoothly. There was no problem.*

Ms Suya further said that she had a son who was in South Africa. When I asked her if he wrote her letters, she said he did not but called her instead. She further explained:

When he calls, we are helped by the young ones here. They tell us which button to press. Everything goes on well without any problems. Even when he writes a message, the young ones read the messages for us. In this regard, although it is important for one to be able to read and write, for us it is too late. We are old.

(Field notes: 18 June 2016)

Ms Suya's stance showed that she was satisfied with the support she was getting from the young ones. With their help, she was not only able to operate the mobile phone but also to get the messages her son sent to her. On the basis of this and the fact that she considered herself old, she saw no reason for enrolling for adult literacy lessons.

Notwithstanding these seemingly positive attitudes towards literacy mediation, there was a sense that some community members had some reservations about the same. For instance, Ms Suwedi cited some practical challenges of getting support saying: *… the problem is sometimes such people are busy*. This meant that the person may not always have their things done within the time frame they wanted. Apart from these practical concerns, some community members, including some of those who benefited from literacy mediation, were bothered by a sense of shame. For example, Ms Duniya told me that she enrolled for the adult literacy lessons because there were occasions when she felt a sense of shame. She said: *I went to Tupoce to receive money and they said that all traditional leaders should sign their names. I asked my niece to sign for me but I felt some shame.* Although Ms Duniya relied heavily on literacy mediation in discharging her duties as a village headperson in her community, she was not happy with the same support in other contexts. She narrated a story in which she and her fellow village headperson went to an official meeting with government officers. At the end of the meeting the village headpersons had to sign for the allowances and because she did not want to print using her thumb, she had to hunt for someone to sign for her which she described as 'humiliating'.

Despite all the challenges which the community members faced with regard to literacy mediation, it remained true that there were many individuals in this community who relied on others, mostly family members, to mediate in some literacy practices they participated in. Thus, although ability to read and write was a key factor and somehow impacted on community members' participation in some activities that required literacy, getting help from others appeared to offer them an alternative access route. Ms Suya's observation about literacy mediation not being a practice for the non-literate persons alone was particularly revealing. This observation, in part mirrored one of the key tenets of the social theory of literacy, that is, the postulation that literacy is not a single entity. Rather, there are multiple literacies and they are context-bound. As such, even those individuals assumed to be literate sometimes need help to function fully in some literacy mediated contexts.

In previous sections, I discussed how artefacts such as money and ration cards constrained community members' participation in various contexts. The discussion in this section has focused on public shame and humiliation some community members felt owing to their failure to sign their names. In the section which follows I focus on two artefacts, namely pens and inkpads which brought opposing feelings to the individuals who employed them.

Literacy artefacts: Pen and inkpad

To sign their names or print using their thumbs, the community members employed pens and inkpads respectively. These two artefacts served across community members' lived worlds, especially in those contexts where one was required to put a mark of one type or the other as evidence of their participation. In this regard, these artefacts provided ways for community members to confirm their participation in activities that required literacy. Secondly, and more importantly, these two literacy artefacts evoked polarized emotions from community members who used them.

Listening to some community members talk about their experiences in certain activities where literacy had a role, there was a sense that pens and inkpads were not just tools one used to acknowledge receipt of either food aid or cash. These artefacts symbolized different worlds to which some community members either claimed or were denied membership. The pen evoked the world of the literate. In this regard, holding a pen was not just a physical act but also a declaration that one was literate. This was the sense I got when some members who were involved in a community savings group told me that the only criterion they use to elect a member as a secretary was that they should be able to hold a pen. At the same time, the pen afforded some community members some pride and respect. For instance, Ms Awali told me that she was no longer interested in acquiring a certificate from her literacy class. Instead

> *I just go there to make sure that I master my name so that when we are called for some other activities, I should be able to sign using a pen. I have already started doing this; even when we were receiving fertilizer coupons, I signed my name. When we went to the Assemblies of God to receive money to buy fertilizer, I got hold of the pen, and they said, 'Grandma, are you going to sign?' I said, 'yes'. They said, 'We respect you!'*
>
> (Field notes: 21 November 2015)

The officers responsible for the programme appeared to doubt Ms Awali's decision to choose a pen over inkpad. The officers perceived Ms Awali as someone who was not able to read and write, and this was why they were surprised to see her get *hold of the pen*, hence the question, *are you going to sign*? And by using the pen to sign her name, Ms Awali earned herself *respect.*

While the pen symbolized literacy and somehow raised the confidence and status of those who could *get hold of it,* the inkpad symbolized 'illiteracy', thereby making those who pressed their thumbs on it as a way of signing feel public shame and humiliation. This state of affairs was exacerbated by the fact that although the inkpad provided non-literate community members opportunities to participate in activities that required writing, some officers had negative attitudes towards it. One of the community members who experienced such attitudes, Ms Suwedi, explained that one of the reasons why some officers did not like thumb printing was that *when you print using your thumb, you spoil their forms because the ink spills over on to the lines others were supposed to sign in.* For some women, the feeling of shame and humiliation they encountered from such experiences was profound, as Ms Faki explained

> *Sometimes I print using my thumb but I feel ashamed. Others are using a pen to sign their names and I am using a thumb print, it is shameful. As you leave, you feel like*

the earth is going to open up and swallow you up. Now I am slowly learning how to write my name.

(Field notes: 28 May 2016)

The contrast between the feelings emanating from the use of the two artefacts comes out very clearly. While one could walk with their head up after using a pen, the other felt like the world was crumbling under their feet after using the inkpad.

However, not all community members appeared to be publicly ashamed of thumb printing, that is, the inkpad. Some such as Ms Suya saw it as a norm.

This is what we have been doing all these years. When they call us, they know that we are old. So, they grab our hands and make us print using our thumbs. Sometimes those who attend literacy classes write things that are not legible and the officials say, 'You have not written anything meaningful here. Just print using your thumb.' Which one is more shameful than the other, to just go and print using your thumb straight away or to be told to print using your thumb after being stopped from signing?

(Field notes: 18 June 2016)

Ms Suya appeared to suggest that the pen did not always afford respect to those who used it. Rather the admiration was earned through competence. As Ms Suya put it, an unsuccessful attempt at using the pen brought with it damaging consequences. Notwithstanding her seemingly positive attitudes towards the use of inkpad, there was a sense that she was just being pragmatic, because as the discussion continued, she said:

we can go and enrol for adult literacy classes. But for us to be able to write is something I do not believe that it is possible. Our hands are a bit feeble. I do not think that we can handle the pen.

(Field notes: 18 June 2016)

What this suggested was that Ms Suya thought that the pen was best suited for the relatively young community members as opposed to the individuals considered to be old whose hands were *feeble*. To some extent, this implied that she did not have any other option than using the inkpad owing to her perceived old age.

Conclusion

The aim of this chapter was to explore the literacy practices and the artefacts some community members encountered in various figured worlds. My emphasis was not on providing detailed accounts of the figured worlds such community members participated in, rather it was to describe how some community members navigated through the literacy practices and artefacts privileged in those figured worlds. In this regard, the discussion has revealed that community members encountered varied and multiple literacy practices facilitated by different and sometimes complex literacy artefacts. As such, the discussion poses a crucial question as to whether the one size-fits-all type of literacy teaching and learning which was taking place at the Sawabu literacy centre was sufficient. This question emanates from the fact that the figured worlds discussed in this chapter emphasized some literacies that were not at the centre of the national adult literacy programme.

Some community members navigated through the various literacies and artefacts with little or no problems at all, owing to mainly three reasons. First, the tasks which required reading and writing in these figured worlds did not oblige them to read and understand the artefacts. Secondly, community members regularly received some literacy mediation from others. Third, thumb printing was sometimes acceptable. However, literacy support and thumb printing were not simple and straightforward processes. These two practices raised some practical, emotional and self-image matters that the community members had to grapple with. This was the case because both practices forced the community members to expose their literacy identities in public, thereby undermining their social status. In this regard, although getting support and thumb printing allowed community members to participate in some literacy practices privileged in their lived worlds, they did so at a cost.

5

Identities and Power in Reading and Writing Spaces

This chapter explores how certain literacy practices and discourses positioned some adult literacy learners in different figured worlds. Such positioning not only contributed to the way the learners perceived themselves but also facilitated or constrained their participation in some activities where reading and writing were required. In their own words and beliefs, the community members saw themselves or others as 'the educated/the uneducated', 'the knowledgeable/the not knowledgeable', 'the intelligent/the struggling', 'the instructor/the learner'. In the sections which follow these pairs are discussed by employing concepts such as positioning, authoring, agency and cultural models (Holland *et al* (1998) and Davies and Harré's (2007) ideas of interactive and reflexive positioning (for more details on these concepts, see Chapter 2). The data I use in this chapter are mostly based on semi-structured interviews, informal interviews/conversations and participant observation in the classroom.

The educated and the uneducated

At Sawabu literacy centre, the learners frequently assigned themselves or other learners the subject position of the 'educated' or the 'uneducated'. They did this by looking at the individual's ability to read and write. Thus, those adult literacy learners who they assumed could read and write were interactively positioned or they reflexively positioned themselves as 'the educated', while those they regarded as being unable to read and write were assigned or claimed the subject position of 'the uneducated'. Such positioning was not surprising because the adult literacy learners' primer explicitly states that *ophunzira m'sukulu za kwacha ndi anthu a zaka ... amene sanapeze mwayi wophunzira*[1] *kale* (the learners in adult literacy classes are individuals who did not have an opportunity to learn/study/be educated in the past). Hence, the two subject positions were influenced by such discourses.

It should be pointed out however, that the subject positions many adult literacy learners were assigned to or identified themselves with were never rigid. Rather, they were fluid. In fact, it was noted that although the community members usually accepted the subject positions assigned to them by others, sometimes they re-authored them. This was the case with Ms Msosa.

Ms Msosa was a widow. She had eight children, seven sons and one daughter. However, all the seven sons had passed on, leaving behind a number of grandchildren. Only the daughter was still alive. Ms Msosa withdrew from primary school in grade 3 because she said she had frequent disciplinary cases with the school authorities emanating from her numerous fights against her classmates. The fights were caused by the teachers who told the other pupils to laugh at her whenever she failed to read in class. She had previously joined an adult literacy class in another village but the lessons were discontinued because the instructor married and went away with her husband. She joined the literacy classes again because she wanted to be able to read the Bible. In the excerpt which follows, she explained more about her literacy learning experiences

Researcher:	*When you look at yourself and the other literacy learners, do you think you are at the same level?*
Ms Msosa:	*No, we are not and I am surprised that they mix us. Some of those literacy learners are 'educated.' They are able to read everything. Now, some are not able to read anything. They do not know even 'a.' So, what I see as a problem is that they just mix us. They do not separate us as grade ones, grade twos, grade threes etc. All of us are put in grade one. This is why there is confusion.*
Researcher:	*Confusion?*
Ms Msosa:	*Yes, there is confusion. You see some literacy learners do this while others do that. For me, I see that Ms Mkakosya, Ms Afiki, Ms Balala, Ms Abasi, are doing much better. These should have been promoted to a different level and that would be understood. These women know everything and they can even teach us. But the rest have a long way to go.*
Researcher:	*So where is the problem in putting everyone in one class?*

[1] This word has multiple meanings, that is, learn, study or be educated.

Ms Msosa:	The problem is that the literacy learners I have mentioned may feel that they are not going forward. Reading the same book they already know is not good for them. You know someone who withdrew from primary school in grade 5 go to the literacy class with a view of continuing with their education. They want to go beyond grade 5. Those women who withdrew from primary school in grade 3, 4 and 5 can be put in the same class. But you cannot combine them with those who have never attended formal education. They should not combine them with the women who do not know even 'a.' These ones should be in their own class. This is what I feel.
Researcher:	You have said that those that are able to read and write are 'educated'; can you explain this?
Ms Msosa:	Yes, they are. There is a difference between those that are not able to read and those that are able to do it. Those that are able to read are educated, there is no question about it.

(Field notes: 5 February 2016)

Here, Ms Msosa suggested that she was not getting enough help due to the practice of putting together literacy learners who, she thought, were at different levels. She also noted that the tendency of learning the same content each year was making those learners she said were 'educated' think that they were not progressing. This was the case because individuals who withdrew from primary school in grade 5 went to the literacy classes to continue with their education and therefore it was wrong to teach them together with beginners. She expected a hierarchical classification of the adult literacy learners into grades. She saw the practice of using the same board, the same space and same instructor to teach different content from the same primer to different sets of learners as confusing.

Ms Msosa was worried about the plight of those learners who, she said, enrolled for the lessons with a view to continuing with their education. What caught my attention though was that she was talking about 'others' and I asked her where she put herself.

Researcher:	You have said that those that are able to read and write are educated; how about you?
Ms Msosa:	No, I do not put myself in that group. I am not educated.
Researcher:	Is being able to read and write the same as being educated?
Ms Msosa:	Yes, there is no question about it.

(Field notes: 5 February 2016)

Generally, Ms Msosa identified and assigned the adult learners including herself different subject positions. She interactively positioned some learners as 'the educated', while the others including herself were positioned as 'the uneducated'. At the literacy class, Ms Msosa was interactively positioned as someone who was not able to read and write; hence, she was *osaphunzira* (the uneducated). In addition, the literacy practices in this context projected her as 'the uneducated'. In one literacy lesson the instructor asked some literacy learners including Ms Msosa to write their names on the chalkboard. Ms Msosa was reluctant to go in front and take part in this exercise. I encouraged her to try. She looked at her notebook so as to see how her name was spelt before going to the board. Ms Msosa wrote 'Ag' and said that she had forgotten. The supervisor asked another literacy learner, Ms Mwenye, to help her and wrote 'Agnes Msosa'. He asked Ms Msosa to copy this in her notebook.

In this case, both the classroom activity and the supervisor positioned Ms Msosa as someone who was not able to write. The literacy activity demanded that everyone involved should write their names from memory. Checking the way her name was written in her notebook was regarded more or less as cheating and, therefore, was not acceptable. With all the other learners looking on, and time being limited, Ms Msosa was not able to complete writing her name. It was incidents like these that led to her being positioned as 'the uneducated', and she seemed to accept this subject position as shown in the extract given below.

Instructor: *Are you trying to copy from your notebook?*
Ms Msosa: *What?*
Instructor: *Are you trying to copy from your notebook?*
Ms Msosa: *But it will disappear. Although I have seen it, it shall disappear.*

(Field notes: 22 October 2015)

Consequently, while some of the adult literacy learners were allowed to enrol for the English literacy classes, she was not, because only those learners who were able to read and write in Chichewa, that is, 'the educated', were eligible for that class.

However, despite both the literacy practices and the literacy officers interactively positioning her as 'the uneducated' because of her inability to read and write, Ms Msosa's actions sometimes suggested otherwise. In fact, she told me that she had a book which she sometimes read. She brought out the book, and as I flipped through it, she 'read' all the words and stories on the pages I had some interest in, including the ones shown in Figure 15. The book appeared to be a literacy primer or a primary school text but it was difficult to tell because all pages which carry bibliographic information had been torn off.

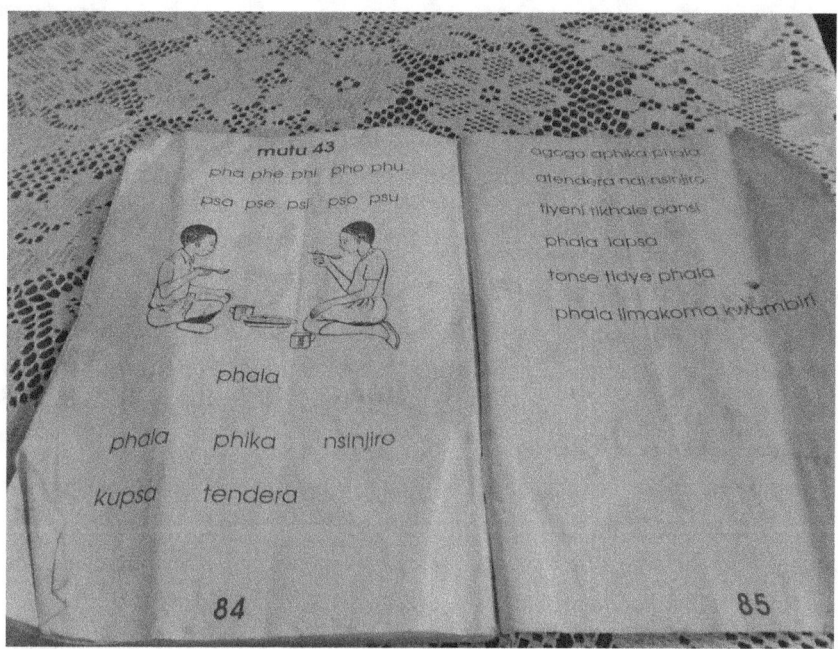

Figure 15 Ms Msosa's Book

Ms Msosa 'read' the words on page 84 as well as the short passage on page 85. By doing this, she reflexively positioned herself as 'the educated'. Thus, in a different context she re-authored her literacy identity. She claimed that the perceived reading problems she encountered at the literacy centre emanated from the stories found in the official literacy primer.

Ms Msosa:	So, some people said, 'Take this book and when you have time read it.' It has 'a, e, i, o, u.' They said if you do not know these things, you will not progress in school. I am able to read in some areas of this book.
Researcher:	Is that so?
Ms Msosa:	Yes. But when I go to the literacy class, I note that what I read here and what we learn there is different.
Researcher:	You mean the letters are different?
Ms Msosa:	No. The letters are the same. They are not different. But the stories, such as the one that says, 'A Beni afufuza bizinesi.' (Mr. Ben searches for a business).

(Field notes: 5 February 2016)

Ms Msosa attributed her observed failure to read and write at the adult literacy class to perceived differences in literacy artefacts. What was significant in all this, though, was the fluidity of Ms Msosa's subject positions. At the literacy class, the literacy practices and the literacy officers interactively positioned her as the 'not able to read and write', and therefore, 'the uneducated'. At home, she 'read' her book to me, thereby projecting herself as someone who was able to read.

While Ms Msosa's opposing subject positions emerged in two different lived worlds, other learners such as Ms Balala displayed opposing subject positions even within the same figured world. Ms Balala was one of the women Ms Msosa interactively positioned as 'the educated'. She was a single mother who withdrew from her primary school in grade 6. She enrolled for the literacy classes because she believed that there were some other things she needed to know which she had not learnt in school. In other words, she saw these classes as one way of continuing with her education.

However, in the literacy class, Ms Balala sometimes reflexively positioned herself as someone who had not yet mastered the reading and writing skills. In one of the lessons, she was asked to write some words on the board, but she declined saying: *sinditha* (I am not be able to do it). In fact, on several occasions Ms Balala refused to be separated from the other literacy learners and be given her own slightly more difficult tasks suitable for 'the educated', saying, 'I will learn together with everyone.' In this regard, Ms Balala not only showed solidarity with her colleagues but also exercised her agency and reflexively positioned herself as one of the 'uneducated' who needed the instructor's attention.

Paradoxically, Ms Balala's actions on other occasions suggested that she reflexively positioned herself as *the educated*. Regularly, Ms Balala complained that she was robbed of the opportunity of being an actor in the figured world of Social Cash Transfer Programme. She said that she was registered during the preliminary registration process which she said marked her eligibility for the programme. However, her name was not on the final list, and she continuously complained about it as I illustrated earlier.

Ms Balala told me that she was now *educated* and therefore she could not be cheated that her name was missed by the computer. She therefore said that she had confronted the officers from the other zones, and they confided in her that it was officers from her own area who were responsible for her name's omission.

It should be pointed out that, although Ms Balala was a woman, the deletion of her name did not seem to suggest that her gender played a part. The officer responsible for the programme in this community, who was also a woman, said that the registration process had two phases. The first one, in which Ms Balala took part, involved collecting data from probable beneficiaries. The data gathered were punched into the computer which was programmed to code it.

The second phase was then the actual identification of beneficiaries in which the said computer used the coded data to select the individuals based on pre-programmed set of criteria.

Because she was positioned as 'the educated' (those able to read and write), Ms Balala had opportunities to hold elected positions. During the elections of a literacy class committee, she was elected secretary. She was the secretary for the People's Party area committee, and also secretary for the tap committee in her neighbourhood. It can be argued that her being positioned as *the one able to read and write* (*the educated*) allowed her not only to participate in, but also to occupy positions of influence in various figured worlds.

The knowledgeable and the not knowledgeable

Although the subject positions of 'the knowledgeable' and 'the not knowledgeable' were used interchangeably with 'the educated' and 'the uneducated', the two dichotomies had some noticeable differences. 'The knowledgeable' and 'the not knowledgeable' encompassed more than the adult literacy learners' ability to read and write. In Chichewa, 'the knowledgeable' were described as *odziwa chichilichonse* (which could literally be translated as 'the all-knowing') and 'the not knowledgeable' were regarded as *mbuli/osadziwa chilichonse* ('the ignorant').

Even though none of the learners I interacted with called themselves *mbuli*, they usually saw themselves as such prior to attending the adult literacy classes. That is, they consistently framed their identities in two ways. Prior to enrolling for the literacy lessons, their identity was generally projected negatively compared to the one they identified themselves with after joining the classes. For example, Ms Kalako said that before attending the classes, she did not know anything. In the same vein, when the supervisor talked about Ms Maulidi's status prior to enrolling for the literacy lessons, he usually positioned her as 'the not knowledgeable', and Ms Maulidi generally accepted this literacy identity as the extract which follows shows:

> *Ms Maulidi:*   It is true that time I did not know anything.
> *Researcher:*   Anything?
> *Ms Maulidi:*   Yes, I did not know anything at the time I was enrolling for the literacy lessons.
> *Researcher:*   Is that so?

Ms Maulidi:	Yes.
Researcher:	*I have always been surprised that you have been consistently mentioned as someone who did not know anything.*
Ms Maulidi:	Yes, I did not know anything and I have been attending the literacy lessons for three years now.
Researcher:	*I see.*

(Field notes: 28 November 2015)

Ms Maulidi thus consistently positioned herself as 'the not knowledgeable' prior to attending the literacy lessons but she felt that things had changed. She was now able to 'read and write'. She said that she was happy that she was able to sign her name.

In some instances, the learners positioned some of their colleagues as more knowledgeable than others. In the extract given earlier, Ms Msosa identified Ms Mkakosya, Ms Afiki, Ms Balala and Ms Abasi as the adult literacy learners who 'know everything and they can even teach us'. Some of the classroom practices confirmed Ms Msosa's observations. For instance, when solving arithmetic problems, the supervisor always insisted on the need to follow laid-down mathematical procedures; he usually asked the learners to explain how they got their answers. Such practices positioned those learners who were able to explain their answers as *the knowledgeable,* whereas those who could not were seen as *the not knowledgeable.* Apparently, driven by their desire to play out their subject position as *the knowledgeable,* two literacy learners, Ms Balala and Ms Imani, wanted the supervisor to explain why, in the problem given below, when we borrow 1 from 3 and bring it to the 2, we get 12 and not 3.

K532.00
<u>-69.00</u>
───────

The debate that ensued suggested that these two learners reflexively positioned themselves as 'the knowledgeable', and interactively positioned the others as 'the not knowledgeable'. The supervisor was very reluctant to answer the question but Ms Balala did not relent.

Ms Balala:	*What is the value of the 1 (one) we borrow from one number and bring it to the other? I notice that the number becomes sometimes 11 or 12, why should 1 make the other number become 11 or 12?*
Supervisor:	*If we were to explain the issue you have raised, then we would confuse the others.*

The response given by the supervisor somehow reinforced Ms Balala's claim to the subject position of 'the knowledgeable'. The supervisor said it was the 'others' who would be confused, not her. Ms Balala's insistence on this matter originated from the questions her colleagues asked her in class. During class work, she was regularly busy explaining to others how to deal with the problems given. Therefore, she appeared to be convinced that she was fighting for those who needed help.

> Ms Balala: No, just make it short. Just say that the 1 we take from there, OK, can I just explain it?
> Supervisor: OK, say it yourself.
> Ms Balala: Should I say it?
> Supervisor: You have asked a question, so that you should be answered.

Here the supervisor appeared to be in a dilemma. He gave Ms Balala permission to explain to her friends what was involved but realized that he was abdicating his responsibility as a teacher. Thus, the power relationships that I shall demonstrate in Chapter 6 came into play. In this case, the supervisor appeared to remind Ms Balala that by asking the question it implied that she did not have an answer, and therefore it did not make sense that she should be the one answering it. In a way, the supervisor was trying to bring Ms Balala back to her perceived subject position of 'the not knowledgeable'. However, Ms Balala continued to resist it.

> Ms Balala: I am deliberately keeping it to myself.
> Ms Imani: So, have you failed to answer the question, sir?
> Supervisor: (Laughs) I have not failed.
> Ms Balala: When we take that 1 and bring it to 2 it becomes 12. These others do not know how this happens.

Ms Balala made it clear that she knew the answer to the question she had asked and that the explanation she was seeking was for the benefit of others, not her. To show her knowledge, she explained the gist of her question. She was then joined by Ms Imani who saw the supervisor's reluctance to answer the question as lack of knowledge and therefore wanted him to admit it. The question Ms Imani posed threatened the position and credibility of the supervisor. He had either to admit failure or provide the explanation they were demanding, and he chose the latter.

> Supervisor: The 1 we take there has the value of what?
> Ms Imani: 10

Supervisor:	It is 10. When we add 2 to 10, what do we have?
Literacy learners:	12
Supervisor:	What?
Literacy learners:	12
Supervisor:	But let us leave this aside. It can confuse you. Is that understood? Am I right, Ms Balala?

Trying not to concede defeat, the supervisor reasserted his position that the explanation Ms Balala was seeking was beyond the comprehension of, not only the other literacy learners, but of Ms Balala as well, that is, '*it can confuse you*'. Here again, the supervisor tried to position Ms Balala as 'the not knowledgeable'. The answers to the two questions the supervisor asked appeared to be obvious. The aim of the two questions was primarily to stamp his authority as he demanded a 'yes' or 'no' reply. Ms Balala had not only to understand but also to confirm that the supervisor was not wrong. However, Ms Balala did not succumb to the supervisor's positioning.

Ms Balala:	*You are right. But they must know that the 1 has the value of 10. We must know. Yes, we must know.*
Ms Imani:	*Because the others can bring that 1 and add it up to 2 and get 3.*
Ms Mkakosya (learner):	*You know that because you worked out that problem in the past.*
Ms Balala:	*Yes, but the others must know. I am not sure whether I have offended you.*

(Field notes: 22 October 2015)

Even after the intervention of another learner, Ms Mkakosya, Ms Balala maintained that it was not her who was supposed to understand the feared confusion; it was the others who needed to know the value of 1 (one). Then grudgingly, she gave in to the supervisor's positioning, saying '*We must know. Yes, we must know*', implying that she too was amongst those positioned as 'the not knowledgeable'. But she closed the conversation by still positioning herself as 'the knowledgeable' and regretted any offence she might have committed by her acts, that is, '*yes, but the others must know*'.

It is worth pointing out that it was mainly the classroom-preferred procedures of calculating the answers that shaped the positioning of some learners as 'the knowledgeable' and others as 'the not knowledgeable', as illustrated in the episode above. Some of the women who were taking part in these lessons, such as Ms Awali, Ms Mwenye and Ms Gesa, were engaged in small-scale businesses, and they successfully dealt with subtraction and addition in their businesses without necessarily bothering about the procedures highlighted in the encounter above. Sitting outside my rented house, I saw Ms Awali transact her business. She gave out some of her items on credit and knew how much each customer owed her without keeping a written record. When the customers paid part of the money they owed her, she was able to work out the balance mentally.

The struggling and the intelligent

In Sawabu village, adult literacy learning was viewed as a school by both the literacy officers and the adult learners. As such, most of the practices that were valued in a formal school setting were noted at this literacy centre. For example, the learners competed in a quest to show who was more intelligent than the others, and therefore the learners were discursively ranked based on their literacy abilities; those perceived to be doing well during the classes were positioned differently from those assumed to be facing some challenges. Consequently, two subject positions emerged for the adult literacy learners: some were regarded as *mbutuma* (the struggling) while others were said to be *anzeru, mitunda or patali* (the intelligent) as the encounter that follows shows.

Supervisor: When you ask Ms Sumani to mention the letters, you will hear her say 'J' referring to 'A.' Then you wonder as to when did 'A' change to 'J.'
Researcher: Was she here last year?
Supervisor: We started with her when this school began.
Researcher: So, this is her third year?
Supervisor: Yes, but she does not know anything. The only one who seems to show some change is Ms Maulidi.
Researcher: Is that so?
Supervisor: Ms Maulidi was the same as Ms Sumani. She did not know anything. But now she is able to read. She was using her thumb print to receive her fertilizer coupons. Now she is able to sign her name.
Researcher: That is encouraging
Supervisor: Yes. Some people were born intelligent.
Researcher: I see.
Supervisor: The only problem was that she was not able to be educated in the past. But she is changing here. We can actually see that had this one been educated in the past, she would have been somewhere. But there are others who are struggling completely.

(Field notes: 22 October 2015)

The supervisor interactively positioned Ms Maulidi as 'the intelligent', while Ms Sumani was seen as 'the struggling' ('struggling completely'). These subject positions were assigned to these women based on the assumption that, despite starting the literacy lessons in the same year, Ms Maulidi was able to do certain things which Ms Sumani was failing to do. For instance, while Ms Maulidi was able to read the primer and sign her name, Ms Sumani was not.

The supervisor was not the only one who interactively positioned some learners as 'the intelligent' and others as 'the struggling'; the learners themselves did the same, as was the case in the exchange which follows:

Ms Awali:	Their group shall be known. Maybe they shall be in the same group as that of Ms Balala
Supervisor:	No, they cannot be in that group. Those ones are intelligent.
Ms Awali:	Especially our chairlady
Supervisor:	Ms Mkakosya?
Ms Awali:	Yes, Ms Mkakosya is intelligent. Here she just pretends as if she does not know.

(Field notes: 2 November 2015)

Both the supervisor and Ms Awali interactively positioned Ms Mkakosya and Ms Balala as 'the intelligent'. At the same time, Ms Awali indicated that Ms Mkakosya reflexively positioned herself as 'the struggling' by pretending not to know. Ms Abudu made similar observations concerning Ms Balala. She said that Ms Balala was pretending not to be able to read and write and that at the end, '*only we the mbutuma* (the struggling) *shall remain.*' Ms Abudu implied that while Ms Balala and others who were positioned as 'the intelligent' would be graduating from the literacy class, she and her fellow *mbutuma* (the struggling) would still be having the literacy lessons. Observing the learners do certain activities in class, I sensed that some of them reflexively positioned themselves as 'the struggling', based on such activities; this was the case with Ms Kalako.

Ms Kalako was a mother of six children. She got married in 2002. Two of her kids were born during her earlier relationship before she got married. She withdrew from school in grade 1 owing to financial problems. The practices at the literacy centre positioned her as 'the struggling', as captured in the extract which follows.

Instructor:	Ms Kalako, what is this? (pointing at the letters)
Ms Kalako:	J, u, m, a. (naming the letters)
Instructor:	Now combine and read them as a word
(Ms Kalako keeps quiet.)	

Instructor:	There. That is where the problem is. When you go to school, you need to ask questions. Don't be afraid that others are going to laugh at you. This is what school is all about.

(Field notes: 28 March 2016)

Here the classroom literacy practices positioned Ms Kalako as 'the struggling' because she failed to combine the letters J, u, m and a and read them as one word '*Juma*'. At the same time, the instructor unequivocally told her that she had a problem which he attributed to her lack of agency. It is understandable, therefore, that Ms Kalako reflexively positioned herself as 'the struggling' (not intelligent) as shown in the following exchange.

Researcher:	You have been attending these classes for three years now, how would you describe yourself?
Ms Kalako:	It is only that because I am not intelligent but I still continue to attend those lessons. The instructors are good but I think I am not intelligent (laughs).
Researcher:	(Amid laughter) So, where are you now?
Ms Kalako:	I am still as I was. I still fail to read anything.
Researcher:	You mean you are unable to read anything?
Ms Kalako:	I am failing to read the whole primer on my own. Of course, I am able to read some single words or letters but I fail to combine letters or words.
Researcher:	Why is this the case?
Ms Kalako:	Because I am not intelligent.

(Field notes: 26 March 2016)

Here Ms Kalako blamed her perceived lack of progress in learning how to read and write on what she thought was her limited intelligence. As far as she was concerned, '*the instructors are good*' and therefore, if at all there was any lack of progress, it was because she lacked intelligence. She positioned herself as 'the struggling' by saying, '*I am as I was. I still fail to read anything.*'

Paradoxically, she said that she was able to read ' ... *some single words or letters* ....' In fact, the activities performed during the closing ceremony of the class projected Ms Kalako as someone who was able to read. She 'read' a paragraph from the official primer fluently and her colleagues clapped hands for her. She also said that she no longer relied on thumb printing. She was now able to sign her name. In this regard, Ms Kalako re-authored her literacy identity from 'the struggling' to 'the intelligent'. Besides, the results of the national adult literacy exams showed that she had passed and, therefore, she was declared 'literate'.

The classroom literacy practices gave more space to those learners who were positioned as 'the intelligent' than they did to those projected as 'the struggling'. For instance, most of the reading activities were primer-based, and the standard practice was that the instructor read the passage first while the adult literacy learners listened. Thereafter, the instructor appointed some learner to read a few lines from the passage. Usually it was those learners who were positioned as 'the intelligent' who did the reading, whereas those seen as 'the struggling' did the listening. Routinely, the literacy learners who were listening did so without even looking at the passage being read. In other words, the classroom practices created some de facto literacy roles for the learners, in that those positioned as 'the intelligent' were the readers and those seen as 'the struggling' were the listeners. The official adult literacy primer reinforced this scenario because most of the scripted reading activities stressed reading the passages fluently so that the messages they carried should be understood. Such a practice gave very little room for the learners positioned as 'the struggling' to experiment with their perceived limited reading skills.

Although one may not question the fact that the adult literacy learners were not gifted equally, there were other factors which the officers or the learners did not consider when assigning themselves or others any of these subject positions. For instance, almost all the learners who were interactively positioned as either 'the educated' or 'the intelligent' had attended primary school and withdrew in or above grade 4, a class that is used as a yardstick for literacy attainment in Malawi. Generally, these were the same learners who passed the 2015 national literacy exams at this centre. The opposite was generally the case with those learners who were interactively positioned or who reflexively positioned themselves as either 'the uneducated' or 'the struggling'. These learners had done less than half or no primary school education at all. Almost all those learners positioned as 'the uneducated' or 'the struggling' failed their 2015 national literacy exams and, therefore, were not declared 'literate', except Ms Dailesi and Ms Kalako. The former withdrew from school in grade 1 but passed the exam, while the latter withdrew in grade 4 and failed it. Notwithstanding this, the general trend showed that there was a systematic relationship between educational background and being positioned as either 'the intelligent' or 'the struggling', including how the learners performed in exams.

It should be noted though that, apart from educational background, other factors such as work and age played a part in making some learners struggle with their learning. In the following exchange, Ms Ndemanga, the stand-in instructor, suggested that Ms Abasi was struggling with her literacy learning because she was too busy.

Ms Ndemanga:	Maybe Ms Abasi is too busy with her business. I think she does not read, am I lying against you? She does not have interest in reading.
Ms Abasi:	I read at night
Ms Ndemanga:	Why then are you failing to combine the letters and form words?
Ms Abasi:	I just forget
Ms Ndemanga:	No.
Resident instructor:	It is possible, because people learn differently, am I right? What we need to do is to screen the prospective literacy learners by establishing how far they had gone with their primary school. Then we decide where and how to start from with the class. So, the problem is with us instructors. We should not hide our shortfalls. We make shortcuts.

(Field notes: 23 November 2015)

Apart from showing that the two literacy officers did not agree on the reasons why Ms Abasi was struggling with her learning, this extract also revealed that the two differed on how to handle adults. Thus, although the resident instructor knew that Ms Abasi was struggling in class, she chose to put the blame on the instructors and not on the learners. The resident instructor knew that blaming Ms Abasi would make her feel ashamed which would in turn demotivate her.

Another reason that made some learners struggle was poor sight owing to old age. Ms Awali, Ms Matiki, Ms Faki and Ms Duniya all complained that they were having problems reading from the primer because of poor eyesight which they blamed on old age. Consequently, the practices privileged in the classroom positioned them as 'the struggling'.

Notwithstanding all the other factors, educational background seemed to matter most. This was the case because in terms of being busy, it was not just Ms Abasi who was doing business. Ms Mwenye and Ms Afiki too were busy and often missed literacy lessons, but they were not positioned as 'the struggling'. The two were doing well in the practices promoted in the class. And there were some learners who were relatively young, such as Ms Dailesi, Ms Tweya, Ms Sumani, Ms Usi and Ms Maulana, who were also positioned as 'the struggling'. In other words, struggling cut across ages. But none of the literacy learners who had done their primary school up to grade 4 and above was positioned as 'the struggling'.

Instructors and learners

Sometimes, the learners positioned themselves and each other in terms of 'instructor' and 'learners'. They did this by comparing the literacy and numeracy competencies of each other. The learners who did classroom activities with ease were sometimes thought to be literate enough to be instructors while those who struggled were said to be learners.

Normally, each adult literacy centre in Malawi is run by one facilitator or instructor. Sawabu literacy centre was slightly different. The supervisor whose residence was in this community helped in facilitating literacy lessons whenever the resident Chichewa instructor sought permission to be absent from duty for a prolonged period of time. The supervisor also instructed an instructor from a dysfunctional literacy centre to be helping at Sawabu centre while arrangements were being made for a new centre to be opened for her. She helped in facilitating Chichewa literacy lessons. The presence of multiple instructors gave the learners an opportunity not only to position the instructors against each other, but also to position some of them against the learners themselves.

Overtly, the learners positioned their instructors as *good*. However, in private, the supervisor said that some of the learners thought that one of the instructors was not good enough to facilitate the lessons. He said: '*The literacy learners were telling me that some of them were far much better than her.*' The supervisor's comments somehow explained the tussles that sometimes emerged, especially when the instructor concerned took charge of the lessons. Some of the learners who (Ms Msosa said) ' … *know everything and they can even teach us*', sometimes implicitly showed that they were indeed better than the stand-in instructor, as seen in the extract that follows.

Stand in instructor:	We apply manure early if it should turn into soil …. They are saying if manure should turn into soil, not so?
Ms Afiki:	so that it should turn into soil
Stand in instructor:	We must make sure that the manure is applied at each maize planting station, not so?
Ms Afiki:	so that it should turn into soil.
Stand in instructor:	it should turn into soil, not so?
Ms Afiki:	They have written that 'we apply manure early, so that it should turn into soil'
Ms Mkakosya:	You have said that 'if it should turn into soil'
Stand in instructor:	Where?
Ms Tepani:	Here. Below. It's getting messed up

Stand in instructor:	'… we apply manure early so that it should turn into soil.' I have already read that part
Ms Mkakosya:	that is not what you said. Just below there 'so that it should turn into soil' but you said, 'if it should turn into soil'
Stand in instructor:	Is that so?

(Field notes: 19 November 2015)

Although one would say that the instructor had made a mistake and that the learners were just trying to correct it, their insistence to have her realize that she had made a mistake suggested that they wanted to show her that they knew how to read the text better than she did. The instructor tried to play down the mistake but the three learners, all of whom were positioned as 'the educated' and 'the knowledgeable' by their colleagues, were determined to have their concern heard. Before this episode, the supervisor had hinted that because of the presence of women such as Ms Mkakosya, Ms Afiki, Ms Balala and others in the class, one would be making a mistake to facilitate literacy lessons without being prepared. Some may be tempted to suggest that the three women behaved the way they did because the instructor was a woman. This may not be entirely correct, because such incidents never occurred when the Chichewa resident instructor who was also a woman presided over the lessons. In any case, the arithmetic incident, cited earlier, suggests that gender was not a major underlying factor. Whenever they saw it necessary, some of these women reminded the instructors that they were not entirely 'illiterate'.

And it was evident that these women knew the discursive subject positions above. Ms Balala categorically said: '*We are at different levels but our colleagues do not understand this. What they say is that these are instructors.*' She said that she was not bothered that her colleagues identified her as such, '*because it is true. If they are failing to write "a" but I am able to do it, then it means I can teach them how to write "a."*' It was not just the learners who elevated some of their colleagues to the status of being *instructors*; some of the instructors shared these views. Ms Ndemanga, the stand-in instructor, openly said: '*Let me tell you. In this class, we have people who are able to read and write such as Ms Balala and others. When the instructors are absent, do not just disperse and go home. These women should go in front and teach.*' The instructor clearly positioned Ms Balala and others as being capable of facilitating literacy lessons, hence interactively positioning them as 'instructors'.

To some extent, the classroom literacy practices too positioned these women as individuals who deserved such a subject position. On a number of occasions, the learners were asked to volunteer or were appointed to lead in some activities such as solving arithmetic problems. In most cases, it was those learners positioned as 'the educated' or 'the intelligent' who volunteered or were appointed to lead, and they did well, as was the case with Ms Afiki. She was asked to lead her colleagues in working out the following arithmetic problem.

```
K27.20
 ×7
 ───
 ─────────
```

Ms Afiki:	Let's do this problem. It involves Kwachas and Tambalas (Malawian money similar to pound and penny) and it is a multiplication problem. 7 x 0.
Other learners:	0.
Ms Afiki:	Now we go to the next number 7 x 2, or we should say two sevens put together.
Other learners:	14.
Ms Afiki:	Are we going to write 14 as a whole?
Other learners:	No.
Ms Afiki:	What are we going to write?
Other learners:	4.
Ms Afiki:	Now because we have kwachas and tambalas, what are we going to do here? (pointing at the space in front of 4).
Other learners:	We put the point.
Ms Afiki:	The problem continues, 7 x 7?
Other learners:	49.
Ms Afiki:	Are we going to write 49 as a whole?
Other learners:	No.
Ms Afiki:	What are we going to put?
Ms Mkakosya (learner):	We are going to add the 1 we kept from the 14 and add it to 49 and together it shall be 50.
Ms Afiki:	And are we going to write 50 as a whole?
Other learners:	No.
Ms Afiki:	What?
Other learners:	0.
Ms Afiki:	What have we kept?
Other learners:	5.
Ms Afiki:	7 x 2.
Other learners:	14.
Ms Afiki:	Let's add to 14 the 5 we kept.
Other learners:	19.

Ms Afiki:	*Are we going to write 19 as a whole?*
Other learners:	*Yes.*
Ms Afiki:	*Have we finished?*
Other learners:	*No.*
Ms Afiki:	*What should we write?*
Other learners:	*'K.'*
Ms Afiki:	*Have we finished or not?*
Other learners:	*We have finished.*
Ms Afiki:	*It means this is our answer not so? (K190.40)*
Other learners:	*Yes.*

(Field notes: 9 November 2015)

Ms Afiki was very comfortable playing out the role of the instructor. Somehow, these practices made the learners who were positioned as 'the instructors' stand out in class. The other learners such as Ms Msosa, Ms Sumani, Ms Duniya and Ms Awali never volunteered to lead in solving such problems. Even in cases where the instructors dared them to try, they always declined, thereby reflexively positioning themselves as 'learners'.

The example given above shows the relatively rare occasions in which the instructors promoted peer learning. The instructors used similar approaches to build the confidence of the learners in public speaking, arguing that:

> *Some of us are required to speak in public and this starts in school like here. When you are asked to speak in public you shall not be shy, just staring at the ground. This is why we ask you to come in front to teach each other. So, when you are in company of others, you are brave. When they say, 'Ms Imani, do this', you would not say, 'I shall not be able to do that', because you already started doing it in school.*

(Field notes: 23 March 2016)

However, in the literacy class, bravery depended on one's literacy and numeracy abilities. In this regard, it was mostly those learners who positioned themselves or were positioned by others as 'instructors', 'the intelligent' or 'the knowledgeable' who had the courage to volunteer and lead others in lesson activities because they had the requisite knowledge and competencies to deal with the issues the class was discussing.

Conclusion

Many literacy theorists and experts share the view that literacy is intertwined with power and identity (see Street, 1993; Collins & Blot, 2003; Papen, 2005; St. Clair,

2010). What this suggests is that any study of literacy and literacy learning is in part about exploring the power relationships and literacy identities that come into play in social encounters where literacy has a role. Understanding these issues is critical because, as this chapter has shown, literacies have the potential of either empowering or disempowering individuals in such encounters. How different literacies are promoted and valued within or across figured worlds influences how the participants position themselves or are positioned by others.

This chapter has shown how a focus on 'power-in-literacy' (Collins & Blot, 2003) reveals not only the interconnection between literacy learning and power and literacy identities but also the fact that literacy identities are never fixed. This fluidity of literacy identities underscores, among other things, the key principle of the social theory of literacy which calls us to recognize the fact that we do not have just one literacy, rather we have multiple literacies. Suffice to say that whenever they wanted, these adult literacy learners exercised their agency to re-author their literacy identities which somehow signalled some form of power struggle; this is the focus of the next chapter.

6

The Adult Literacy Class: A Site of Power Struggle

When the term 'power' is mentioned, it generally evokes a binary between those who have it and those who do not, thereby creating an impression that power is a 'commodity' that can be possessed. In a formal classroom situation this perception usually emerges especially when the teachers wield power over their pupils. Thus, teachers generally take charge and control what pupils do in class. Such power relationships are usually anchored by rules and regulations such that offenders are sanctioned. But importing these practices into a non-formal literacy learning context sometimes creates tensions between the learners and their instructors.

This chapter focuses on what was seen as struggles for power involving the literacy officers, the instructors and the adult literacy learners at Sawabu literacy centre. Specifically, I look at the extent to which the decisions affecting literacy learners' interests were influenced by power relationships amongst the officers involved in the delivery of the literacy lessons. In addition, I also look at how some social tendencies which I call 'school culture' gave more authority to the instructors and diminished the learners' agency in the decision-making processes. As explained in chapter two, although my account focuses primarily on Lukes's (2005) perspectives of power I am aware that power as a concept is both complex and contested (see Guzzini, 2007).

It should be remembered that there were four literacy officers working at Sawabu literacy centre. These included the cluster supervisor, the English instructor, the resident Chichewa instructor and a stand-by instructor whose centre had been closed and was asked to be helping at this centre whenever necessary.

Dilemmas of enforcing bureaucracy in non-formal settings

Influenced by my past experiences both as a teacher and a pupil, I went into my fieldwork with an assumption that the power relationships cultivated in literacy classes were very different from what I had encountered in formal classrooms. I had in mind Knowles's (1980) view that 'the andragogical practice treats the learning-teaching transaction as the mutual responsibility of learners and teacher' (p. 48). I therefore, expected to see the learners have some form of control over how the learning process should be conducted. In practice however, my assumption turned out to be incorrect.

The learners at Sawabu literacy centre were involved in many activities to sustain their daily lives. As a result, they had to balance the time they needed for these activities on the one hand and for literacy lessons on the other. Finding that balance proved to be difficult. Consequently, sometimes tensions between the learners and their instructors emerged. This was the case because while the learners sought to prioritize their sources of livelihoods, the instructors were torn between either accepting the learners' position or rejecting it for fear of losing their jobs.

This situation emerged when the rainy season approached and the learners frequently talked about their plans to suspend the literacy lessons. But their request sparked a prolonged argument between the instructor and the supervisor on the one hand and the literacy learners and the instructor on the other. The instructor supported the learners' request but the supervisor opposed it and this put the instructor in a very difficult situation. As an 'employee of the government', she knew that she did not have the power to unilaterally make decisions that affected the operations of the literacy centre. She had to take instructions from officers above her. At community level, she was aware that the literacy learners depended on farming for their livelihoods. So, when the learners pressed her to decide, she sought guidance from the same people who were waiting for her decision, saying: *'The supervisor is not yet back. You are the ones to give me power, because I cannot decide on my own. You tell me what to do.'*

As she spoke, one could feel her frustrations and sense of powerlessness. She felt that she could not act on her own. Her agency was subject to what either the supervisor or the learners authorized her to do. Since the other authority was away and the matter needed urgent attention, hence, *'You tell me what to do.'* But by asking for authority from the learners, the instructor was attempting to put the responsibility for the suspension of the classes squarely in the hands of the literacy learners. In this case if she was queried by her authorities about the suspension, she could tell them that it was the learners themselves who had suspended the lessons and not her. The tension surrounding the issue of suspending the classes contradicted what the supervisor had privately said earlier, when he had indicated that classes were generally suspended in the rainy season.

> Supervisor: *Exams are written in May because during that time, the rainy season, schools are erratic.*
> Me: *Is that so?*
> Supervisor: *Maybe this one will not be disrupted because you have encouraged it. So even during the rainy season, the women will be coming but in other villages it is difficult.*
> Me: *I see*
> Supervisor: *Sir, in other villages the schools are not running smoothly.*
> (Field notes: 2 November 2015)

Here the supervisor acknowledged the problem of holding lessons during the rainy season, although he expressed optimism that classes at this centre were not going to be affected so much, because I had motivated the literacy learners. Although I was aware that since I came to this community, a couple of learners who had withdrawn from classes had re-enrolled for the lessons, I did not understand why the supervisor assumed that my presence had changed the learners' attitudes towards attending classes during a period that was very critical for their livelihoods. Ironically, the learners' sustained request to write their exams early and suspend the classes at the onset of the rains, coupled with the instructor's endorsement of the request, somewhat contradicted the supervisor's assumptions that the classes would continue because of my presence in the community.

When the crops were ready for harvesting, the learners revived their request to suspend the lessons, and the stand-off was re-ignited. However, this time the learners exercised their agency and decided to prioritize their crops over the lessons. Interestingly, despite the learners' absence from the classes, the instructors continued to report for their duties. Sometimes, only one learner turned up but still no classes were held. Tired of what was happening, the English instructor, the supervisor and Ms Mwenye, one of the learners, discussed the situation so as to chart the way forward.

English instructor:	Are we going to learn today?
Supervisor:	People are very busy.
Ms Mwenye:	Sir, people are saying that they were told that there is a two-week recess.
Supervisor:	Is there anyone who said this here?
Ms Mwenye:	When I was coming, Ms Duniya said, 'Where are you going? I thought they said we should be on recess for two weeks?' This news has spread all the way to Cilanga village.
English instructor:	The women did ask that they wanted to harvest their crops first. They have just given themselves that break.
Supervisor:	They have done it on their own?

(Field notes: 11 April 2016)

When I listened to the three discuss the situation, the struggle for power was evident to me. Ms Mwenye's revelation about the suspension of the classes surprised the supervisor, and therefore he wanted to know if there was anyone amongst the officers who had permitted the literacy learners to be on recess. The answer given by the English instructor did not convince the supervisor, hence the question: '*They have done it on their own?*' This question also showed that the supervisor realized that the learners were not as powerless as he had assumed. The key issue here was not the suspension of the classes, because the supervisor knew that '*people are very busy*'; rather it was the realization that someone had usurped his powers and ordered the recess.

However, as the stand-off continued, I began to question whether my presence was not exacerbating the situation. Since it was normal practice for them to suspend lessons during this period, I was wondering as to why they found it difficult to do the same this time around. I wondered whether the supervisor was trying not to disappoint me by carrying on with the literacy lessons. I later discovered that his reluctance to suspend the classes revolved around his fears that the new District Community Development Officer, who was keen on revitalizing the operations of the literacy classes in the district, would come to visit the class without giving notice. The supervisor told the English instructor that '*it is possible for us to close the school but there is a danger. I am not comfortable with those forms that give the location of the school. I am afraid because of that one.*' I realized that if I wanted to gain a better understanding of the power dynamics I was witnessing at this literacy centre, I needed to look at a broader picture, including the role of artefacts. The supervisor's remark revealed that he understood the significance of the adult literacy learners' request, but that he was afraid that his superiors might come to the class unannounced.

The supervisor and the instructor, therefore, agreed not to suspend the classes formally. They resolved that even if a single learner turned up for the lessons, they were going to teach her. To some extent, by making this resolution the two were sending a message to the learners that they did not have the mandate to suspend the classes. However, the English instructor raised some practical concerns regarding this arrangement, saying: '*The challenge I am anticipating is that we have done all these with Ms Afiki [one of the learners] but other learners who have not done these are going to show up one day, what will I do? Should I start [my teaching] all over again?*' In response, the supervisor told her that if Ms Afiki who had not taken a break was present in that class, then the instructor should continue from where she stopped with her. But if she is absent, then the instructor will choose whatever she liked to discuss with them. The supervisor argued that '*even in formal schools, the teachers never reteach lessons for the sake of the absentees. You just copy notes from friends but they are difficult to understand because you were not taught.*' But it can be argued that the approach taken by the supervisor was a form of punishment against the so-called absentees. This stance appeared to be a tit-for-tat, just because the learners had suspended the classes '*on their own*'. In other words, it appeared to be an attempt to reclaim his authority which he felt had been undermined by the learners' action of giving themselves a two-week break without his consent. He justified his stance by referring to what happens in formal schools. Although the literacy learners also perceived their learning as 'school', the rationale of expecting them to behave like school pupils who would be keen to copy classroom notes was rather questionable. In this regard, it was not clear as to whose interests this position was meant to serve.

To conclude, it could be argued that by adhering to rules and regulations to run the literacy class, the learners and their instructors cultivated modes of interaction that created a teacher-pupil power relationship which in some ways impacted on the decision-making processes at this literacy centre. These practices generally thrive on asymmetrical power relationships which, if strictly enforced in a non-formal setting where rules and regulations are followed out of respect, create tensions as suggested earlier. While the presence of more than one instructor helped the learners to have some uninterrupted literacy lessons, it also created some tensions, mainly because the two officers occupied positions vested with different powers in NALP's organizational structure. In this way, the literacy class typified a formal school set-up, whereby the supervisor had more authority than the instructor in the same way heads of schools and teachers do in primary and secondary schools. This 'school' set-up, coupled with the learners' desire to enact their previous school practices, was conducive for the emergence of what I call the 'school culture'.

The 'school culture'

There were many community members in Sawabu village who had enrolled for literacy classes with a view to continuing with their education. For many learners, their literacy class was a 'school', just like any other formal educational institution; as Ms Matiki put it:

> *No, there are no differences. If you go to primary schools, they have a, e, i. o. u, and in classes we also have these. The only difference is that we are not flogged but in primary school when you do something wrong, they flog you.*
>
> (Field notes: 1 April 2016)

From Ms Matiki's perspective, the literacy class was the same as formal primary school. This perception was common amongst many literacy learners. What was intriguing though was not just the perception but rather the attempt to perform school practices reminiscent of those done by pupils in primary school, which I call 'school culture'. Although the learners welcomed the school culture, as the extract above shows, it brought power relationships which, to some extent, muted the literacy learners' voices.

In general terms, when Ms Matiki talked about flogging, she was referring to matters concerning discipline. Although the literacy learners were not physically punished, there were some tendencies of emphasizing discipline just like in formal schools at this literacy centre. The learners sat on the floor in rows, and somehow, they were expected to conduct themselves in the same way pupils would behave in a formal classroom setting. In this way, there were attempts to enact teacher–pupil identities that matched with the 'school culture', as the extract below suggests.

Supervisor [to class]:	*If there is any problem tell me, raise your hand. If you ask each other, then you are making noise. If you ask amongst yourselves, then we will not hear it. If there is a problem about what I am teaching today, raise your hand and I will come and discuss with you. If there is a problem that has nothing to do with the lesson, then wait until we knock off. Is that understood?*
Literacy learners:	*Yes.*

(Field notes: 12 October 2015)

What the supervisor was promoting in this case was a formal school model that gave the teacher the authority to take charge of the classroom proceedings. Whoever wanted to speak could only be recognized if they raised their hand. Seeking help from a fellow learner on the issue under discussion was looked at as making noise, but doing the same as permitted by the literacy instructor was not. When the supervisor posed the question: '*is that understood?*', he was just stamping his authority as a teacher. Nonetheless, despite accepting their instructor's regulations, no learner was seen raising up her hand in order to have the opportunity to speak in class. When they wanted to join in any discussion, they just chipped in.

It is worth pointing out that, while the discipline measures provided order in the classroom, they also limited healthy debates amongst the literacy learners. Restricting learners to discuss any issues they had with the instructor created the impression that learning took place only through the interaction between the teacher and learners, that is, teacher-centred approach. Besides, these measures denied the learners opportunities to socialize. The regulations prevented the learners from sharing the vast knowledge and lived experiences they brought to the class.

Crucially, strict adherence to discipline measures sometimes created tensions between the instructors and the learners, culminating in the latter's voices being silenced. This is what happened to Ms Matiki. One day, she came to the lesson late. As she walked towards where her colleagues were sitting, she jokingly said: '*Late comer, don't worry.*' The instructor reprimanded her immediately, saying, '*We have banned noise making.*' Looking deflated, Ms Matiki said: '*I am sorry.*' Thereafter, she remained quiet and unresponsive. During the lesson, the instructor wanted to know whether or not she was following what was being taught but she did not answer. When pressed further, she inaudibly said, '*Just carry on.*' Yet, Ms Matiki was a learner who was usually very active in answering questions in class.

These tensions also sometimes erupted between the instructors and the class as a whole. This happened especially when the learners were told to do something, they were not ready to do. For instance, just like what happens in primary schools in Malawi, the literacy learners were asked to sing songs as lesson interludes. It was very common to hear the supervisor say: '*Sing songs, do not make noise.*' By 'noise', the instructor was referring to 'talking to each other without being permitted to do so, regardless of the pitch'. Hence, the supervisor saw singing songs as a way of controlling 'noise' amongst the learners. Although the learners often complied and sang the songs, they sometimes resisted as the following example shows.

> Supervisor: Songs are like lessons. They are special lessons. So, as we prepare for the next lesson, you should be singing songs. You get rid of worries through singing songs. I want to write something on the board, so sing songs.
> Literacy learners: (Silence)
> Supervisor: Sing songs.
> Literacy learners: (Silence).
> Supervisor: Should we say the person who leads in singing the songs is absent today?
> Literacy learners: (None of the literacy learners starts a song. Instead, they are chatting as the supervisor writes on the board.)
> (Field notes: 3 November 2015)

Sitting on my bench in the classroom, I felt the tension building up as this episode unfolded. The learners appeared as if they did not hear what their supervisor was asking them to do. They carried on talking to each other as their supervisor, who appeared dismayed by their lack of cooperation, wrote on the chalkboard. When he finished writing, he said: '*Let us stop talking. We have failed to sing songs.*' The supervisor viewed the learners' action as a sign of failure and not resistance. He later said that he would not stop asking the literacy learners to sing songs because, according to him, '*songs were special lessons.*' Suffice to say that he was the only officer at this centre who saw the benefits of singing, as he claimed.

Songs: More than special lessons

Singing songs in the literacy class had broader implications than just being '*special lessons*'. The literacy class was part of the wider community and, therefore, certain things happening outside the class had a bearing on how the literacy learners participated in classroom activities. On one occasion, the supervisor asked Ms Afadi to lead in singing songs but she refused, saying '*I cannot sing. I have just had a funeral recently.*' What this suggested is that Ms Afadi did not see the singing of songs as '*special lessons*' but rather as a form of entertainment. In this regard, she did not want to appear to be merrymaking when her family was still mourning the loss of one of their relatives. Although Ms Balala finally led in the singing of the songs, Ms Afadi did not join in. With her right hand propping up her head below the chin, she just sat there, downcast.

Coming to the class on time was another issue through which the instructors and the literacy learners exercised their power. Although one would understand the reason why the instructors emphasized punctuality, it was somehow surprising that they went to the extent of making a decree that *'If you are at home up to after 3 o'clock, do not come here. We do not want to restart the lessons. We must start together.'* The supervisor justified this decree by showing his displeasure at repeating what they had already said to accommodate latecomers, although this rarely happened. The learners who reported late for lessons just knocked on the door, came in and sat down. What the supervisor did not like however, was the fact that *'You will start asking others, what lesson? By asking others such questions, you cause noise in the classroom.'* But it was not clear as to whose interest the decree was attempting to safeguard. In a village setting like the one we were in, the concept of time was generally problematic, especially among older women who in most cases used the position of the sun to tell time. On many occasions when I arrived at my rented house, I found that Ms Awali, one of the learners, was not yet ready for the classes. Although she had a radio, she usually asked me about the time, and when I told her, she often told me that the sun was still high up. Even when I was allowed to observe their group activities, they rarely started at the time they told me. Therefore, although punctuality was important to the instructors, it was doubtful that the decree was going to work. In fact, even after this order was given, the women came for the lessons at the times they thought were convenient to them. When on one occasion Ms Gesa came late and was asked to be punctual, she said that she was busy with some work and that when she finished, she decided to go to the class, saying to herself, *'Let them send me away.'* I saw Ms Gesa's action as a form of open defiance to the decree. This encounter underscored the fact that enforcing punctuality rules in a non-formal setting in the same way as one would do in a formal school environment was problematic. On this particular occasion, all the instructor had to say to Ms Gesa was: *'You are not going to be sent away. It is better to come late than being absent.'*

Having noted the complexities that were emerging as the instructors tried to enforce some disciplinary measures at the literacy class, I asked one of the instructors if there were any rules, and if there were, who made them? In response, she said: *'The school has some rules. For instance, we tell them to be punctual. We tell them to be disciplined in class.'* The instructor's language revealed a master-subservient relationship. That is, it suggested that the role of the instructors was to issue instructions, and the learners were supposed to obey, that is, *'We tell them ....'* The instructor claimed that the rules were made by the literacy school committee in collaboration with the instructors. But the learners suggested otherwise, as I found out from Ms Gesa and Ms Matiki. In the extract which follows, the former saw me at the latter's house and she came to find out what was happening because it was customary that lessons were not held on Friday.

Ms Matiki:	This is what I was asking. I was wondering as to whether we are going to be having lessons on Fridays.
Ms Gesa:	Maybe he just came for a visit (referring to me).
Ms Matiki:	Maybe things have changed?
Ms Gesa:	Maybe
Ms Matiki:	But do you think people would be coming for lessons on Fridays?
Ms Gesa:	It is possible
Researcher:	Who makes such changes, the instructors or the literacy learners?
Ms Gesa:	It is the instructor
Researcher:	They are the ones who say we should be holding classes on these days?
Ms Gesa:	Yes. They announce in the class. Maybe the other learners were told.

(Field notes: 1 April 2016)

Knowles (1980) cautions that teachers should not take the 'school culture' the adult literacy leaners display 'at face value and start treating [them] as if they were dependent personalities' (p. 46). But changing such behaviours proved to be very difficult. In fact, Ms Matiki once said that '*at school, there is always someone in authority, sometimes a headmaster.*' Thus, even in some cases when the instructors asked the learners to state what they wanted to learn, the latter pushed the responsibility of selecting the content back to the instructors, saying, '*That is how things should be.*' When they occasionally attempted to state what they wanted to learn, they restricted themselves to picking issues from their literacy primer. They identified topics they said they found difficult to comprehend. Yet going around the community and listening to what many people, including the literacy learners themselves, said, there was a sense that signing one's name dominated their discourse. But they did not ask the instructors to prioritize this literacy practice, because doing so would go against what they believed to be the school norms.

School and expectations

Perceiving the adult literacy classes as 'school' not only cultivated the complexities discussed above, but it also brought about frustrations amongst some literacy learners. Some community members who attended classes at Sawabu literacy centre already knew how to read and write before coming for the lessons. Some of them said that they went to the classes to 'continue with their education'. However, there was a sense that the class failed to satisfy their aims. Consequently, they became frustrated, as Ms Imani narrated.

Researcher:	You said you joined the literacy classes to continue with your education, is there anything specific you want to learn?
Ms Imani:	Yes. I want to learn English. As for Chichewa, I am able to read and write certain things.
Researcher:	What do you need English for?
Ms Imani:	There are certain jobs that require English. Sometimes visitors come and you fail to communicate with them because you do not know how to speak English.
Researcher:	So, what jobs do you aspire to?
Ms Imani:	Any other job
Researcher:	It has been three years now since you started attending the literacy lessons, do you think your aim is being achieved?
Ms Imani:	No, it is not being achieved. I am just learning Chichewa. Also, I am not being promoted to another class. They do not say, 'You are going to the next class.' This means that you are still in the same class. In primary school, you write exams as we do in the literacy class; if you pass you go to the next class. If you remain in the same class, it means you have failed and therefore you are repeating the class.
Researcher:	Should I say you view the literacy class as being the same as primary school such that when you pass you move on to the next level?
Ms Imani:	Yes, we should move to the next level. They should say, 'You have passed, go to this class.' But we are writing the exams and remain in the same class.

(Field notes: 29 February 2016)

Ms Imani's frustrations were palpable. She too perceived the literacy class as 'school', hence her comparison of the literacy class to primary school. Ms Imani's complaints suggested that as a 'school', the literacy class did not live up to her expectations. She expected the literacy class to have more than one subject. In addition, she expected to see many classes, so that learners could be promoted from one class to another. According to her, being in the same class and learning the same content every year meant that '*You have failed and therefore you are repeating the class.*' What this suggested was that the notion of 'school' brought up some hope to Ms Imani to continue with her education. But she was frustrated that her goal was not being achieved. These frustrations were heightened further by the fact that the NALP is not linked to formal education.

It is worth pointing out, though, that both the literacy instructors and the officers at the district office were aware of the frustration facing the literacy learners. The instructors said there was need to screen literacy learners during the registration exercise to establish the grades at which they withdrew from primary schools. They said that once that was done, '*Then you determine how to proceed with your class.*' Similarly, officers at the district office said that the literacy learners were sometimes separated. '*Those literacy learners who seem to be ahead are put on one side and those that are lagging behind are put on the other side of the room.*' But neither of these was done at this literacy class. In any case, even if such screening and separation had been done, such acts may not have helped in addressing Ms Imani's frustrations. They may have helped in addressing practical concerns regarding the teaching and learning of literacy but not resolving matters of promoting learners from one class to the other. In fact, since this was a government literacy programme which was primer-based, the different groups that would be identified in the class would be taught using the same primer every year. This would result in the same frustrations of being in the same class and being taught the same content, as Ms Imani had put it.

What is evident from the discussions above is that the idea of looking at the literacy class as 'school' in the same way as formal education cultivated false expectations among some of the learners. This is why some learners thought that their exams had the same value and purpose as those written in formal schools. In the extract above, Ms Imani equated writing exams to being promoted to another class. At the same time, other women such as Ms Usi saw passing such exams as a way of getting a certificate that would help her get a job. '*It could be a job I never expected because it is the certificate that will act as evidence that I am educated.*' But as Ms Awali and some literacy officers at the district office put it, such expectations were far-fetched. Ms Awali let her frustration and despair known, when she said:

> *I do not see any benefits from those exams. If I may tell you, I started school long time ago. In those days my sight was good. I attended literacy classes for 6 months. We wrote the exams and I received a blue certificate which I have misplaced. They said, 'This one has benefits.' I put it in my suitcase. I said, I may use this to get a job as a cleaner. But it did not have value. It was just getting worn out in my suitcase. I have not heard that there is anyone who got employed using that certificate. I just go there to make sure that I master my name, so that when we are called for some other activities, I should be able to sign using a pen.*

(Field notes: 11 February 2016)

Ms Awali told me how she admired hospital cleaners. She said that she longed to push the trolleys and serve food to patients. She explained to me how happy she was when she received her literacy certificate. She thought that her dream was going to be fulfilled. She waited for her opportunity to come until she realized that her certificate '*did not have value*'. Thus, Ms Awali decided to change her focus to at least master her name, so that she was '*able to sign using a pen*'. That was the goal she was still pursuing when I found her. She appeared to be satisfied with this goal and she was receiving praises from many people including the village headperson for being able to sign her name in various social activities. Ms Awali's observation about the value of the certificates was echoed by some officers at the district office who said: '*Those certificates are just honorary.*'

A critical look at the discussion reveals that the 'school culture' was not a fixed norm. It was a practice which was subject to reinterpretation. While the instructors had power vested in them by the office they occupied, the learners were not naive to do whatever their instructors directed them to do. They had some agency which, when exercised, threatened the 'school culture' they sought to play out. For instance, the learners suspended the literacy lessons without the authority of their instructors. They continued to chat in class despite being constantly told to keep quiet. They resisted singing songs when they were not in the mood to do so. They came to the literacy class at the time that was appropriate to them despite pleas from the instructors for punctuality. In view of this, it can be argued that although the 'school culture' muted the voices of the literacy learners in some ways, it may be fair to say that the muting reflected respect rather than inability to act. The literacy learners tried to maintain a cordial relationship with their instructors by allowing them to take a lead in decision-making. But the learners had the ability to draw the red lines for their instructors not to cross, hence the power struggle. Overall, the learners were not oblivious of what the literacy lessons would help them achieve.

We will go, let them send us back

Generally, the adult literacy learners enrol for lessons voluntarily to fulfil their own purposes. As such, decisions concerning what kind of literacy one should learn are ideally supposed to be in the hands of the individual concerned. The supervisor confirmed these assumptions when he said that the literacy learners would be given the freedom to choose whether to be in an English or Chichewa literacy class once the lessons resumed. However, on the day of registration, the instructors placed a restriction for enrolment into the English class but the learners questioned the rationale behind it.

Supervisor:	How are we going to divide ourselves?
Ms Upile:	You mean we should have one group learning Chichewa and the other one learning English?
Supervisor:	Yes.
Ms Upile:	But those of us learning Chichewa literacy also want to learn English. Just like school children, they learn both English and Chichewa, we too want the same.
Supervisor:	The policy for adult literacy is that we must have just one subject. This is why you receive just one primer. It is not possible to teach both English and Chichewa to same group. Those literacy learners who will be in the Chichewa literacy class will not attend English literacy classes; the same will be the case with those in the English literacy class.

(Field notes: 8 March 2016)

Ms Upile, who identified herself as a Chichewa literacy learner, did not support the idea of splitting the class into two. As a Chichewa literacy learner, Ms Upile knew that if the division was done as suggested then she would not be able to learn English. Other learners supported her views. She therefore suggested a formal school model where time was allocated to various subjects. To her, such a model would provide equal opportunities to all. But according to the supervisor, the formal school model was not in tandem with the adult literacy 'policy'. The instructors argued that a literacy learner who had not yet gained the writing and reading skills in Chichewa cannot be placed in the English class. The instructors' argument echoed the views of the literacy officers at the district office who were involved in the training of English literacy instructors. During the training, the trainers told the trainees that the 'policy' regarding English literacy was that only Chichewa literacy 'graduates' were to be enrolled for the classes. But these learners candidly challenged this 'policy', saying: '*We will go and let them send us back. We will see from there. Should we fail, we have nothing to lose.*'

Through their words, the learners exercised their agency and showed their determination to get what they wanted regardless of the instructors' regulations. The learners directly challenged the authority of the instructors, including the 'policy' they talked about. During informal conversation some weeks before the registration exercise, the literacy learners talked about and questioned the rationale behind using Chichewa literacy as a prerequisite for learning reading and writing in English. At that time, they argued that children in nursery school were taught English before they knew anything about reading and writing, and therefore, they did not see any reason why Chichewa literacy was regarded as a yardstick for enrolling in the English class (I discuss literacy and language issues in detail in Chapter 7).

When the registration exercise finally started, the learners were allowed to choose the class they wanted to be in, as the supervisor had earlier stated. However, things changed again when some of the learners deemed to be ineligible for the English literacy lessons submitted their names to be in that class.

Supervisor:	Who wants to be in the English literacy class?
Ms Afiki:	I am one of them. Write my name.
Supervisor:	Who else?
Other literacy learners:	Ms Imani,
Ms Sanatu:	Ms Sanatu
Ms Upile:	Ms Upile
Supervisor:	In English literacy class?
Ms Upile:	Yes
Supervisor:	I think you should start in a Chichewa literacy class

(Field notes: 8 March 2016)

By posing the question: '*In English literacy class?*' the supervisor did not just want to confirm what he had heard but also cast doubts about Ms Upile's eligibility as an English literacy learner. This question was an indication that to him Ms Upile was not fit to be in that class, hence his suggestion, '*I think you should start in a Chichewa literacy class.*' The supervisor was exercising his authority to judge Ms Upile's capabilities to place her in a class he thought best suited her. In so doing, he was inadvertently or otherwise inhibiting some learners' access to the literacies they wished to learn. Conversely, when Ms Upile answered, '*Yes*', I saw it not just as a confirmation of what she had said but also as an assertion that she had the right to be in the English literacy class. In other words, she was exercising her agency which sent a clear message that she knew what was good for her.

After the registration exercise, the supervisor confided in me, saying, '*Some of those that have decided to be in the English class such as Ms Upile will go back to Chichewa class. She is just too proud of herself. She is not able to read and write properly in Chichewa.*' These remarks gave me the impression that the supervisor was not happy with the decisions made by some of the women. He substantiated his claims by sticking to his assumption that Chichewa literacy was a prerequisite for learning reading and writing in English. It should be stated, however, that the learners were not asked the kind of English skills they wanted to learn. Despite the literacy classes emphasizing reading and writing, privately the women said that they wanted to learn how to speak English in relation to their lived worlds. The English literacy instructor confirmed this during an informal conversation:

> Researcher: *What aspects of English are you teaching?*
>
> English instructor: *At the moment I started with level 2 book 1. What we have done so far is how to welcome someone at your place. The women said that before I taught them anything, they wanted to know how to welcome a customer in their businesses. So, I just touched on this one.*
>
> Researcher: *I see. You did what they wanted.*
>
> English instructor: *That's right. They told me not to bother about writing. They said that when an English-speaking person comes to their business benches, they are unable to talk to them. Instead they call other people to assist them. So, they wanted to know how to welcome customers.*
>
> (Field notes: 11 April 2016)

This conversation made me believe that the learners who went to the English class had multiple agendas. What was striking to me was how these literacy learners employed their agency to achieve their goals. These were the same learners who indicated that, as a school, it was the instructors who had the responsibility of deciding what they should be taught. What this meant was that their apparent inability to suggest to the instructors what they wanted to learn could not be explained by just power relationships alone. Their felt needs mattered too.

Conclusion

The community members came to the literacy class to learn how to read and write. But unlike children, they brought with them not only their ages and immense experiences (see Chapter 8) but also their desire to make up for their lost school opportunities. As such, the learners sometimes displayed behaviours reminiscent of school children, which I call 'school culture'. While the 'school culture' seemed to have been helpful in some ways in making it easier to run and control the teaching and learning process, it sometimes ran the risk of giving too much power to the literacy officers. This chapter has shown how this culture limited the space for learners to interact freely and make decisions aimed at advancing their interests. In addition, it also placed the power to decide who should learn what kind of literacy largely in the hands of the instructors and supervisor. But wielding 'power over' learners in an initiative they joined voluntarily created a power struggle between the officers and learners, as the latter sometimes exercised their agency. Thus, the learners had the capacity to resist and even defy the authority of their instructors to pursue their own interests. I would therefore argue that, despite promoting the 'school culture', the learners were not naive to accept whatever their instructors dictated. Their perceived school was subject to reinterpretation and was generally underpinned by mutual respect.

Part of this tension was caused by the tendency to enforce bureaucratic practices in a non-formal initiative. The chapter has shown how strict adherence to the officers' bureaucratic positions hampered decision-making processes. The instructor could not close the 'school' without the consent of the supervisor who in turn could not do the same without the knowledge of his superiors. We have seen how the presence of an official form made it difficult for the instructor and the supervisor to act decisively, thereby creating tensions not only between them and the learners but also between themselves. The challenge for the literacy instructors, though, was how to balance between allowing the learners to play out their school-like identities and at the same time recognizing the fact that they were not school children.

7

'Mbecete M'ciyawo': Language Use in Literacy Classrooms

Although scholars and literacy experts understand that literacy in whatever form cannot be taught or studied without referring to a language, deciding which language or languages should be used in adult literacy classes in a multilingual setting appears to be both difficult and contentious (see UNESCO, 2010; UNESCO, 2003). This is the case because considerations of classroom language involve decisions regarding not only which language(s) would facilitate literacy learning better but also issues of power, culture and identity (McCaffery, Merrifield, & Millican, 2007).

In Chapter 6, I discussed how the learners failed to understand why literacy competence in Chichewa could be a prerequisite for learning English literacy. This chapter takes that discussion further by focusing on classroom language use. My fieldwork experience made me understand that the question of which language should be employed in a literacy class in a multilingual setting is much more complex than just choosing between either using the dominant languages or the mother tongues. I saw how the learners struggled to express themselves in a classroom because they were forced to use a language they could not speak properly, as shown in the extract below, prompting me to think that the use of mother tongue would have been the best practice. At the same time, I heard the literacy learners say they wanted their class to be the same as a formal primary school where paradoxically the language they struggling to speak, Chichewa, was the only local language recognized as a medium of instruction.

As I stated in Chapter 3, this study employed multiple techniques to collect data. As such, the data I am using in this chapter are based on classroom participant observation, semi-structured interviews and artefacts.

On one occasion, I observed the literacy learners discuss how to make drinking water clean and safe. The instructor asked one of the learners to explain in Chichewa why a cup was placed on the water bucket and another one was hooked to a nail on the wall.

Ms Sumani:	One is supposed to be put aside, the other one is supposed to be put on the pot
Instructor:	The other one is for what?
Ms Sumani:	One is supposed to be hung on the nail, the other one is meant to be put on the pot
Instructor:	The one that is put on the pot is supposed to be used to do what?
Ms Sumani:	we should take the other cup, the one the woman is holding, we should draw water and put it in, and draw water which is in the pot, 'mbecete m'Ciyawo' (should I speak in Ciyawo?) (Field notes: 30 September 2015)

As I watched this episode unfold, I began to understand why the issue of language of instruction in adult literacy in a multilingual setting in general and in the NALP in Malawi in particular requires serious attention.

Drawing on data like this, this chapter illustrates how different literacies such as the acquisition of specialized knowledge and the learning of specific literacy practices may require different languages within the same literacy classroom. It shows how language use in a literacy class may vary by considering the language(s) privileged by the socially and culturally created activities in which the literacy learners seek to operate, which I frame as figured worlds on the one hand and the kinds of literacies being learnt on the other.

Language of the classroom in a multilingual context

Skutnabb-Kangas and McCarty (2006) construe multilingualism as having two levels, namely individual and community or state level. The two authors view multilingualism at individual level as 'involving proficiency in and use of two or more languages by an individual', whereas multilingualism at community or state level is 'when two or more languages are widely used in a community or state' (p. 2). (See also UNESCO, 2003, cf Kaplan & Baldauf, 1997.).

As I stated in Chapter 1, there are about sixteen local languages spoken across Malawi (Centre for Language Studies, 2006 & 2009) and Chichewa is the majority language followed by Ciyawo and Citumbuka (Kayambazinthu, 2003).

In terms of geographical distribution, Chichewa with its varieties Chinyanja and Chimang'anja, and Ciyawo have many native speakers in both the central and southern regions of the country while Citumbuka is predominantly spoken in the northern region.

Given the multiplicity of languages in the country, many Malawians speak at least two languages. At Sawabu literacy centre, for example, many literacy learners were bilingual, that is, they spoke and understood Ciyawo and Chichewa although during informal conversations they spoke mostly Ciyawo. But as highlighted in Chapter 4, the community members encountered more than the two languages in their everyday literacy experiences. It is complexities like these which make some experts pay attention to issues such as the purposes for literacy, what the learners want to read or write, the local literacy context and the resources set aside for the programme (McCaffery, Merrifield & Millican, 2007) when thinking about classroom language(s). What this means is that the learning of literacy not only 'build[s] on the communication patterns of learners' but also helps them to use literacy 'in ways and for purposes that they themselves define' (Robinson, 2014: 5). Besides, as Martin-Jones (2000) writes, 'languages and literacies are crucial symbolic resources for negotiating new relationships and for constructing new identities' (p. 150).

National language policy in Malawi

Historically, Malawi's national language policy has been shifting since the colonial era. In 1918, a junior Government officer resurrected the idea that the Nyanja language (now Chinyanja) should be made the official language of the country and that it should be taught in all its schools (Vail & White, 1989). The Christian missions, especially Livingstonia, resisted this policy and the result was that in 1947, Citumbuka became an official language alongside Chinyanja and remained so up until 1968.

After Nyasaland, now Malawi, became independent, its urgent task was to seek social-cultural integration and self-reliance, and to achieve this it was felt necessary to minimize linguistic diversity (Kishindo, 1994). So, when the Malawi Congress Party (MCP) held its annual convention in 1968 in Lilongwe, it strongly recommended that in the interest of national unity:

(i) Malawi [should] adopt Chinyanja as a national language
(ii) that the name Chinyanja [should] henceforth be known as Chichewa

(iii) that Chichewa and English [should] be official languages of the state of Malawi and all other languages would continue to be used in everyday private life in their respective areas (*Malawi Congress Party Convention Resolutions, 1965–1983*) cited in Kishindo (1994).

This state of affairs remained so throughout Malawi's one-party state until 1994 when a new political dispensation came into effect. Unlike in the one-party era, where emphasis was put on national unity, and any form of diversity was perceived as a threat, the new multiparty democracy saw any form of pluralism as a resource. Thus, in the new Malawi the emphasis was not just on unity but also on promoting and safeguarding people's human rights.

Defining language as a human right meant that the national language policy had to change as well. Hence minority languages began to be tolerated in some official contexts such as public radio, although the 1968 MCP resolution continues to be the country's de facto national language policy. Thus, although minority languages are tolerated in some official figured worlds, especially the state-controlled radio station, Malawi Broadcasting Corporation, their inclusion has been the result of presidential directives rather than a systematic language planning process.

Policy on medium of instruction in adult literacy in Malawi

Malawi's current National Functional Adult Literacy Programme has undergone several changes since it was first introduced in the country in 1986. However, throughout these changes, not much attention has been given to issues of language of instruction although the important role of the medium of instruction in this initiative is often acknowledged. Thus, the choice of the medium of instruction in adult literacy in Malawi has been influenced by the changes made in the national language policy. Since its launch, the NALP in Malawi has employed Chichewa as the sole official medium of instruction and the choice of this language was based on the 1968 national language policy (Rokadiya, 1986). The rationale for this choice was twofold. First, it was assumed that the use of this language in teaching literacy would promote culture. Second, it was assumed that employing this language as a medium of instruction in this programme would foster national integration. The current shift in the national language policy of allowing other local languages in some official figured worlds is also being considered in adult literacy. This is evident in the Ministry of Education's (2007) new draft Language in Education Policy which stipulates that:

> The overall objective of the policy ... shall be to have as many adults as possible who are functionally literate in their languages so that they can contribute meaningfully to the country's socio-economic development. To fulfil this objective the policy shall promote the learning of basic reading and writing skills through familiar local languages.

However, no further details are provided. A similar stance is also made in the Government of the Republic of Malawi's (2007) draft National Adult Literacy Policy which stipulates that:

> The Ministry shall promote the use of local languages in the delivery of adult literacy programmes since research shows that mother tongue allows creating (sic) teaching in a familiar language while giving learners an active choice about the language in which they would like to learn.

What this means is that when these policies are ratified, languages such as Ciyawo, Cilomwe and others may be used as media of instruction in adult literacy.

But a close look at these two draft policies reveals subtle but significant differences. For example, the Draft Language in Education policy promotes the use of 'familiar local languages' while the Draft National Adult Literacy Policy calls for the use of 'local languages'. The key difference here is the presence of the word 'familiar' in the former and the absence of the same in the latter. Although both policies do not state what they mean by 'local', promoting the use of 'local languages' as the Draft National Adult Literacy Policy stipulates does not address the purported language problem squarely because even Chichewa which is currently used and is reportedly said to be causing problems is a local language (see Chinsinga & Dulani, 2006). At the same time the Draft National Adult Literacy Policy is using terms such as local languages, mother tongue and familiar languages interchangeably as if they meant the same thing. The problem of this practice is that some of the terms such as mother tongue have multiple connotations. For example, mother tongue may mean 'language(s) one learns first, identifies with, and/or is identified by others as a native speaker of; sometimes also the language that one is most competent in or uses most' (Skutnabb-Kangas & McCarty, 2006: 7). Despite the controversies surrounding some of the terms such as mother tongue and local language, I am using them in this book because they appear in the policy documents I have cited and I do not intend to engage myself in the debates.

The policy changes in the language of instruction stipulated in the two draft documents are based on consultancy reports on adult literacy which allude to the fact that adult learners whose mother tongue is not Chichewa face problems in class when instruction is carried out in this language (see Chinsinga & Dulani, 2006). However, no specific and relevant studies on the linguistic needs of the adults have been made to assess whether this policy shift was necessary. In fact

> since 1966 population census, no research has been done nation-wide to ascertain patterns of languages use. As a result, so little is known with certainty about these patterns and what influences them, as *sine qua non* for policy making in education, rural and urban development programmes.
>
> (Kishindo, 1994: 104)

The need for such studies cannot be overemphasized, especially when we consider the fact that adults enrol for literacy classes to achieve their own aims. Hence, making a one-size-fits-all pronouncement on which language should be used in an adult literacy classroom may be contentious. In fact, many literacy experts acknowledge that 'the presumed cognitive advantage of learning a first literacy in one's mother tongue may be small relative to the motivational aspects of learning to read in the second language' (Wagner, 1992: 63). It is also noted that 'without a certain scale of usage, a written language may be of limited utility and its mastery of little appeal to its speakers' (Ryan, 1985: 160). The key issue here appears to be relevance, because literacy is not just 'a skill to be learned for its own sake', (Mipando & Higgs, 1982: n.p.) but rather a fundamental element which is required to facilitate the desires of the learners.

Paradoxically, lack of relevance has been cited as one of the reasons why the adult literacy programme is not making adequate progress in Malawi. Phiri and Safalaoh (2003) note that the adult literacy programme in Malawi is failing to attract the required numbers per class and that it is experiencing a high turnover because of, among other things, lack of perceived benefits after graduation. Perhaps this relevance may be achieved partly by striking a balance between addressing pedagogical concerns attested and the functionality of the literacy the learners would learn.

Languages of the classroom in formal and informal contexts

A critical look at how decisions concerning medium or language of instruction in adult literacy classes are handled appears to suggest that literacy experts generally do not differentiate between how such a language operates in formal schooling and in adult literacy. In formal education, the language of instruction is understood simply as a language that is used to teach 'something'. In this case, the 'something' is the content such as agriculture, geography, history etc. Understood in this way, the medium of instruction becomes the 'vehicle' through which the content is passed on to the learners. This is why education experts advocate the use of mother tongue, that is, the language the learners are most competent in and use most (Skutnabb-Kangas & McCarty, 2006) especially in lower primary school.

However, with adult literacy, the situation is very complex. Thus, whether mother tongue should be used or not depends on a number of factors because, even in Malawi where the NALP is informed by the autonomous model of literacy, the learners are not exposed to a single literacy. Rokadiya (1986) lists four components of the NALP curriculum in Malawi, namely reading, writing, numeracy and functional knowledge. Broadly, this content may be collapsed into two, namely, 'literacy as reading and writing' and 'literacy as functional knowledge'. One of the literacy officers at the district office made this distinction clear when he said:

> *Our programme is called functional adult literacy. Why the word 'functional?' It is functional because what we want is a result-oriented programme. The aim is not that our graduates should get employed. We want them to do in their homes what we teach them in class. At first, materials were being developed taking into account the local needs. For instance, those along the lake, their primers focused on fishing or rice growing. The aim was that once they are able to read and write, they should appreciate the things that are within their local areas. It is noted that many people do not go to school in Malawi. The economy of this country depends on agriculture and unfortunately the majority of the people who do farm work are those that have not been to school. This is why we have issues concerning agriculture, health, family planning etc.*
>
> *Our major aim is to see a change in behaviour in our literacy learners. We want to see that they are doing what we teach them in class. 'Has she or he absorbed something from the class? Is she/he practising it at home?' The reading and writing are secondary.*
>
> (Field notes: 22 June 2016)

Here, the district literacy officer made it explicit that the goal of the NALP in Malawi is to promote certain kinds of social change. It is for this purpose, therefore, that the programme introduces the learners to various issues in a wide range of areas, including health, agriculture, environment, gender, income generation and good governance. As is the case with similar programmes elsewhere, most of the issues covered in the programme centre on what the learners already do or do not do. The programme's major concern is not social transformation whereby there is a 'shift in social relationships [affecting] all forms of social interaction, and all individuals and communities simultaneously' (Castles, 2015: 4) but rather a limited view of social change which aims at bringing into order those individuals perceived to be departing from the assumed universal norms. The challenge, therefore, is for literacy planners to decide which language(s) can facilitate proper communication between the purported change agents, the literacy instructors and the assumed change seekers, the learners. Since social change hinges on issues which the literacy learners already know and do, the decision on which language becomes the medium of instruction is based on whether the best practice is the use of a language they employ when they do such things in their daily lives as the National Adult Literacy Policy stipulates in the extract above or employ the one they struggle to speak and understand in class.

Teaching literacy as functional knowledge

In many African countries including Malawi, the choice of language of instruction in adult literacy programmes is generally spearheaded by other underlying agendas, some of which are not primarily about literacy per se. In some cases, such choices are informed by the quest to promote culture and national unity (see Rokadiya, 1986; Maruatona & Cervero, 2004). In others, it is informed by the desire to promote and protect languages and language rights (see Robinson, 2014).

Since the goal of the NALP in Malawi is to make rural populations conform to what the programme designers perceive as the standard and acceptable practices, the programme appears to assume that the shift in the language of instruction policy as cited earlier would facilitate especially the teaching and learning of literacy as functional knowledge. In this case, the aim of using a language the people already speak as a medium of instruction is to facilitate easy understanding of the issues which generally interrelate with the learners' lived experiences. It is hoped that in this way bringing about change in behaviour would not be a matter of telling the learners what to do but rather engaging with them in honest discussions which may bring forward the reasons why they do certain things the way they do, and at the same time it would allow them to understand why they need to change. In fact, questions are sometimes asked as to whether it makes sense that learners learn things such as how to prepare meals using a language they struggle to speak and comprehend. It is argued that this tendency usually mutes the learners and, in the process, makes them appear as though they had never before done the activities being discussed. This is what we see in the episode about making drinking water clean and safe as cited in the introduction earlier. That episode showed that to some extent, the learner had some knowledge about the need to have the two cups but she 'lacked a language' to express herself. One would therefore be hesitant to conclude that Ms Sumani's failure to provide the answer which the instructor expected was a manifestation of her lack of knowledge. Ms Sumani knew that the answer she had provided was not good enough. She also knew that the reason why her answer did not meet the instructor's expectations was her lack of command of the Chichewa language, hence her request to be allowed to speak in the language she was most competent in and used most, that is, *'mbecete m'Ciyawo?'* (should I speak in Ciyawo?).

This was not the only time that Ms Sumani requested the instructor to be allowed to speak in Ciyawo. She did so on many occasions. What was interesting to me was that in all those instances, Ms Sumani made her request in Ciyawo, not in Chichewa, which to some extent sent a clear message to the instructor that the use of Chichewa in discussing issues affecting her life was limiting her participation in such deliberations. Sometimes Ms Sumani chose to contribute in classroom discussions using Ciyawo without the instructor sanctioning it.

In one of such occasions, the instructor asked the learners to mention the things depicted in the illustration for the day's lesson. Ms Sumani offered to answer the question and identified one of the things as *'ngokwe'* (granary) in Ciyawo. The instructor was not amused by this and quickly said, *'Should we be speaking in Ciyawo in this class?'* In this encounter, it was apparent that Ms Sumani's answer was turned down, not because it was factually inaccurate but rather because she used a language not sanctioned by the programme. Ms Sumani was asked to repeat her answer in Chichewa but she just kept quiet.

Listening to the learners talk when the instructor was preparing to switch lesson activities, I was amused to note that they did not use Chichewa as the language of the classroom. Even when they sometimes wanted to query privately what the instructor had said, they did so in Ciyawo as I witnessed in the episode below.

| Instructor: | We also plant different crops, not so? We plant potatoes, am I right? So, they are telling us that when we harvest our maize, we should plant other crops that would help us avert hunger. So, we can plant potatoes or cassava. As you know, potatoes are nsima.[1] But most of us when we eat |

---

[1] Hard porridge made mainly with maize flour.

>   *potatoes we behave as if we have not eaten anything until*
>   *we eat nsima.*
> Ms Matiki to Ms Msosa: *Ana mbatata sila ugali? (Are potatoes nsima?–Laughter)*
>   (Field notes: 18 November 2015)

Besides, even when they occasionally approached me to check or mark their work, they never spoke to me in Chichewa. All they did was to ask me in Ciyawo, '*ana ngombwele ambuje*' (have I got it right sir?).

On the surface, these encounters may tempt one to suggest that if the reason for using Chichewa is purely pedagogical and not acquisition planning, that is, organized efforts to promote the learning of a language (Cooper, 1989: 157), then mother tongue instruction is ideal when teaching 'literacy as functional knowledge'. It appears that such a practice would help learners like Ms Sumani to participate freely in classroom discussions. That is, apart from helping such learners to meaningfully engage in classroom deliberations, mother tongue would help them relate what they are learning in class with their lived experiences. Making such connections is very important because it helps the learners understand that the issues they discuss in class revolve directly around their lived experiences and not the '*things just written in the books*' as another community member, Ms Awali, once observed.

However, the situation is not as straightforward as it appears to be. In Chapter 6, I discussed the fact that some learners equated their literacy class to formal schools. In this regard, they expected their class to do the same things and to have the same features as formal primary schools. What such expectations suggest is that using any language other than the one used as a medium of instruction in formal schools, especially in lower primary, may frustrate such learners.

These episodes also reveal the paradox of the language of the classroom in relation to power. In Malawi, Chichewa is an official language alongside English, hence to some extent it is a language of power. Therefore, its choice and use in adult literacy among speakers of other Malawian languages could be perceived as an attempt to empower them because it would help them access crucial information and also enable them to communicate with the wider community. In practice, the use of this language in the literacy classroom appeared to disempower some learners and, in some cases, led to classroom power struggles similar to the ones I discussed in Chapter 6. In the encounter cited in the introduction for example, Ms Sumani sought permission to use Ciyawo because she knew that it was only the instructor who had powers to sanction the use of other languages in the classroom. At the same time Ms Sumani's silence when she was asked to repeat her answer in Chichewa could be seen as either a sign of lack of competence in the language or a mark of resistance. In a second encounter, Ms Sumani appeared to resist the programme's monolingual policy by providing her answer in Ciyawo without begging the instructor to do so, thereby disrupting the power relations prevalent in the classroom prompting the instructor to question the use of the language. Thus, although code-switching, that is, the ability to shift from one language to another (Wardhaugh, 1990: 100) was the norm in the daily lives of the learners, it was not tolerated in classroom planned activities.

Teaching literacy as reading and writing

If the choice of one particular language to teach 'literacy as functional knowledge' is contentious, then it is even more problematic when dealing with 'literacy as reading and writing'. This is the case because of a number of reasons. First, 'literacy as reading and writing' is intertwined with language. This is why some language experts view reading and writing as language processes that involve written symbols which represent language (Hudelson, 1994). In short, 'literacy as reading and writing' represents language in a different form. Thus, teaching the learners English literacy is to some extent teaching them English language. So, ideally, when proponents of mother tongue instruction advocate the use of such languages, they are in part promoting the teaching of mother tongues, since 'the expert view is that mother tongue instruction should cover both the teaching *of* and the teaching *through* this language' (UNESCO, 2003: 14). What this means is that if learners were to be taught reading and writing in Ciyawo, then they will have to be introduced to, among other things, the alphabet, orthographic principles as well as the sound systems of the language. This is the case because it would be rather odd to teach the learners how to read and write in Chichewa using Ciyawo as I explain later in this chapter.

One of the general expectations of proponents of mother instruction is that the learners would be able to transfer their mother tongue literacy abilities to other languages. It is observed that the transfer of literacy abilities becomes easier when the writing systems of the two languages are similar. However, although many Bantu languages display many similarities, they also show some differences that would inhibit this transfer in some ways as would be shown later.

Second, adult literacy learners enrol for literacy classes to accomplish their own felt needs. As we saw in Chapter 5, some learners, such as Ms Imani, saw literacy learning as continuing with one's education. Ms Imani said that when the literacy classes were introduced in her community, she decided to join in 'so that I should be able to know some of the things I did not finish learning in primary school'. Thus, to some extent, Ms Imani saw the introduction of the literacy class in her community as another chance for her to go further with her education. Her remarks suggested that she had some unfinished business in as far as her education was concerned. In fact, others such as Ms Maulidi saw their literacy class as *school*, claiming that they learnt things in the same way children in primary schools did. Ms. Maulidi said that her literacy class was not different from formal schools because '*kids go to school to learn how to read and write, we too go there to learn the same in addition to counting our money*'. These sentiments were echoed by another learner, Ms Mkakosya who said:

> *that one is called school because the instructor prepares the content to teach us, reading writing and arithmetic. In that way, it is not different from primary school. In primary school too, the teacher prepares what to teach the pupils, reading writing, arithmetic and English. … When we were going to register for the literacy lessons, we wanted to learn the same things we were learning in primary school.*
>
> (Field notes: 23 July 2016)

Ms Mkakosya justified her school orientation by comparing the experiences learners encounter in the two contexts. In both contexts, the learner is seen as the recipient of the knowledge prepared by the teacher. Besides, the content taught in both worlds was perceived to be the same, that is, reading, writing and arithmetic. She said she enrolled for the lessons because she wanted to learn the same things she was learning in primary school. In short, she wanted a formal school for adults. Certainly, these perceptions have some implications on the choice of language of the classroom in adult literacy, because the formal school setting these learners wanted to cultivate officially tolerates only two languages, namely English and Chichewa. This suggests that the use of mother tongue to teach literacy to learners whose aspiration is to continue with their education may not be appropriate.

Third, the use of mother tongue to deal with 'literacy as reading and writing' may be problematic because people do not just learn to read and write but rather, they learn to read or write 'something'. The adult literacy learners who enrolled for literacy lessons at Sawabu literacy centre were no exception. Ms Awali, for example, enrolled for the literacy classes just because she wanted to learn how to write her name. She said that being able to write her name made her proud because it earned her some respect in some contexts. Ms Suwedi too, said:

For me to be found in that literacy class I had problems. I had problems because I do not like borrowing money from women groups. I go and borrow money from other groups and there they do not accept thumb printing. They insist that one should sign their names. I did borrow the money but in most cases, it was after struggles. They wrote my name on a piece of paper from where I copied on to their forms. They said they did not want any thumb print on their forms. So, when I heard that there was an adult literacy class at Sawabu I said that is good. I should be able to write just my name only.

(Field notes: 24 February 2016)

Although thumb printing also served the purpose, what the women did not like was that sometimes they were scorned for not being able to sign their names and, as another learner, Ms Afiki, once said, '*they looked at you contemptuously.*'

For other community members such as Ms Tweya, Ms Usi and Ms Sanatu, their goal was to learn how to read bus and road signs. The three adult literacy learners said that they did not want to rely on other people's help because '*these days some people cannot be trusted.*' To some extent, what these women wanted to learn represented different literacies which had value in the situations they wanted to operate in. Navigating through such contexts did not involve just one's ability to code and decode the written symbols. It was also imperative for one to be conversant with all the nuances which legitimized such literacies in these figured worlds. For example, one of the placards I saw on a bus operating on the road passing through this area read as follows:

Songani
Malosa

To read and understand the placard one required more than just the ability to sound out the words. The two words were not written in a line from left to right. Instead, one word was written on top of the other. It is this arrangement which provided the words their meaning. On their own, the place names did not say everything you needed to know about how the bus was going to travel. This board did not mean that the bus was coming from Songani heading to Malosa but rather that it was going to Songani first and then will proceed to Malosa. In other words, its starting point was not Songani bust somewhere else. The question here is whether mother tongue or indeed just one language can be used to teach and learn bus and road signs.

For Ciyawo speakers, place names such as Chiradzulu, Mwanza and Livunzu which appear on some bus placards for example, would be difficult to teach using Ciyawo because the alphabet of this language does not have 'R', 'Z' and 'V'. This is the case because Ciyawo, just like Chichewa, is an alphabetic language. Alphabetic languages are those languages which have 'a letter or combinations of letters and marks to represent each speech sound in the language' (https://dictionary.cambridge.org/dictionary/english/alphabetic). In the case of the letters cited above, the Ciyawo alphabet does not include them because they do not have corresponding sounds in the language. For /z/ and /v/ only their voiceless counterparts /s/ and /f/ are found in Ciyawo as seen in the following words, *sala* (hunger) and *fufuma* (bulge). Hence teaching how to read place names on bus placards would require more than using just the mother tongue unless the learners' mother tongue was the same as the one on the placard. In this case, the literacy learners would require the knowledge of the alphabets of other languages to help them read such names.

Similar challenges would be faced when helping learners to be able to read road signs. One of the road signs Ms Maulana, Ms Tweya, Ms Usi and Ms Sanatu encountered within their community was the one shown in Figure 16. This road

Figure 16 Road Sign

sign too showed that learners would find it hard to read it if they were literate in their mother tongue, Ciyawo.

This road sign was not written in Ciyawo, the language which was predominantly spoken by the people in this community. Instead it employed two languages, English and Chichewa. The Chichewa words on this sign literally say, 'We enter songs (put songs); remove viruses; we also teach computer.' So, although the learners had a certain degree of linguistic competence in Chichewa, there was a possibility that they would face some challenges in reading and understanding the Chichewa words on this road sign, let alone the English ones if they had learnt reading and writing in their mother tongue, Ciyawo. Such challenges may emerge because of a number of factors. Just like with place names, they may face problems in sounding out certain letters such as 'V', 'R' and 'Z' because they are not part of the Ciyawo alphabet. In addition, aspiration is not a feature in Ciyawo and therefore, the learners may experience difficulties in articulating some consonantal clusters such as 'ph-' in 'timaphunzitsanso' (we also teach). Besides, some consonantal combinations such as 'ts-, ch-' are not permissible in Ciyawo, hence they would appear novel to the learners if they were literate in Ciyawo.

What these possible challenges mean is that teaching the learners road and bus signs is more complex than it appears at face value. To some extent, it signals what Pemagbi and Rogers (1996) calls the real literacies approach. The real literacies approach recognizes that different groups of literacy learners are involved in different activities that require different literacies in their daily lives. As such 'any learning programme which is designed to help them to develop their literacy skills will need to be different' (ibid: 18). This difference is not just in the kinds of literacies involved but also in the languages employed, since different figured worlds value different languages. Besides, one cannot claim to be teaching real literacies if the languages used to teach those literacies are not the ones used in the materials. The key issue here is to help the learners navigate through the contexts in which they seek to operate because as Bartlett (2008a) observes 'doing literacy is not merely about mastering a code, but largely about developing command of literacy practices that are recognized as "legitimate"' (p. 37).

Conclusion

The issue of which language or languages should be used in the adult literacy classroom in a multilingual context is complex and therefore requires serious consideration. Privileging any language in this figured world is not merely about resolving pedagogical concerns, but it is also about exercising power, refiguring identities and framing political aspirations. This chapter has shown how the use of Chichewa in Malawi's NALP to achieve among other things a political goal of uniting the country has left some learners struggling to learn literacy on linguistic grounds. The chapter has also demonstrated how although the use of mother tongue would facilitate easy learning and enhance the learners' linguistic identity, it may also deprive them of the linguistic capital (Bourdieu (1977) required in figured worlds where their languages do not have value. Although finding a balance among all the factors discussed in this chapter is a daunting task, employing a one literacy one language formal education model in determining classroom languages in adult literacy may certainly create more problems than solutions. The social theory of literacy postulates that literacy is situated. Therefore, adopting a one-size-fits-all approach in resolving issues of language use in an adult literacy classroom in a multilingual setting may be problematic. Proper consultations and flexibility over these issues may be required.

8

Literacy, Power and Identity in Figured Worlds

The hallmark of the social theory of literacy is the recognition of the fact that literacy varies subject to the contexts. In part such variations signal not only how power is embedded in literacy practices but also how literacy identities are never fixed. These identities and power relationships are fundamental because they not only determine who should be included/excluded from specific social worlds but also position individuals relative to each other. In this chapter, I employ my interpretation of Holland *et al*'s (1998) sociocultural theory of self and identity, especially the concept of figured world and related notions which I examined in Chapter 2, to account for the key issues emerging from chapters 4 to 7. The concepts I use include refiguring, power relations, agency, improvisation, resistance, figuring, positioning and artefacts. On positioning, I employ Holland *et al*'s ideas of positionality complemented by Davies and Harré's (2007) adapted characterization of interactive and reflexive positioning. In order to enhance the discussions, in some cases I draw on the materials I used in my previous chapters while in others, I incorporate new ones. My approach involves pulling together key issues that relate to specific notions and discuss them through those lenses.

Refiguring power relations in literacy learning

The Malawi government 'constructs' adult literacy as a process of learning a myriad of 'social goods' (Gee, 1999) which include specialized knowledge, skills, attitudes and techniques. The individuals who are presumed to undergo this process are 'illiterate beneficiaries aged 15 and above' (Government of the Republic of Malawi, 2007). In this way, the government positions itself as the benefactor while the literacy learners are imagined and discursively positioned as individuals in need of help. Although the government literacy policy does not go far in describing who these 'illiterates' are, the primer identifies them as those individuals who did not go to school when they were young. Such are the individuals to be recruited into the figured world of adult literacy learning in Malawi.

In Chapter 1, I observed that the National Adult Literacy Programme (NALP) in Malawi is delivered based on the autonomous model (Street, 1984) in which everyone is expected to learn the same officially scripted content in the same manner as well as in sequence. Once the adult literacy learners master such content, they are expected to employ it in all contexts where literacy is required. Typical of any formal learning programme, the adult literacy learning is evoked by centrally produced artefacts (primers, instructor's guides, attendance registers, examinations, monthly report forms and examination results forms). Significance is given to the teaching and learning of the content outlined in the official documents. At the same time, the passing of the official exams is the outcome that is valued most. In terms of teaching and learning methods, the programme advocates strategies that are ostensibly different from those used when teaching schoolchildren (see Chapter 2).

I went into my fieldwork carrying a number of assumptions about adult literacy teaching and learning based on this official figuring. However, in practice I noted that the community members refigured the world of adult literacy learning into a model which they appeared to cherish. Both the literacy learners and their instructors fashioned their own way of interacting which was in sharp contrast to that figured by the government. To them adult literacy learning was school. As such, they tried all they could to ensure that their literacy class had the identity of a particular formal school and in Chapter 6, I called such tendencies 'the school culture'.

To enact the 'school culture', the literacy learners called themselves schoolchildren and did things as if they were who they said they were (Holland *et al*, 1998). Such a culture brought with it relational identities (ibid) imbued with asymmetrical power relationships. They called their instructors either *madamu* (madam) or *sala* (sir). That way, the world of adult literacy learning was 'peopled by the figures, characters, and types who [carried] out its tasks and who also [had] styles of interacting within, distinguishable perspectives on, and orientations toward it' (ibid: 51). Similar tendencies are reported by Millican (2004) in a South African context. The production and reproduction of this world involved two things. First, my participants employed their school-based knowledge and experiences as their 'significant regularities' which anchored their interpretation of classroom practices. Their behaviour and actions in the literacy class suggested that they were using such knowledge and experiences to interpret what they were doing in this context. Thus, as I demonstrated in Chapter 6, the women either consciously or unconsciously sat on the floor in rows. They sang songs just as I did when I was in primary school. The supervisor insisted that such songs served as lessons despite facing resistance from the learners on a few occasions. They were expected to raise their hands to ask or answer a question. Talking to each other in class was deemed as making noise. They were expected to notify the instructors if they were unable to come for the lessons. They were very eager to have their work marked. Anyone who missed a lesson was to copy notes from those who were present because the instructors were not going to reteach lessons for their sake. At the end of the lessons, the register was called out and the literacy learners answered loudly. In fact, the literacy learners who were attending English literacy lessons demanded that the instructor should teach them 'how to answer the register'.

Within the same 'school culture', other adult literacy learners refigured the literacy classes as a way of continuing with their education. This was the case especially with those adult literacy learners who had done their primary school to a level at which they were able to read and write. These literacy learners such as Ms Imani, Ms Mkakosya, Ms Balala, Ms Mwenye and Ms Afiki refigured adult literacy classes as an avenue for completing what they had failed to accomplish during their childhood education. They employed a school-related discourse model to explain how they expected the literacy classes to operate. They said that since they were writing exams at the end of their literacy learning process, it made sense, therefore, that those literacy learners who 'passed' such exams should be promoted to the next class. They observed that '*if you remain in the same class it means you have failed and therefore, you are repeating the class*'.

Somehow, I was not surprised that these adult learners perceived their literacy class as school because even official documents constructed them as such (see Chapter 1). Hence, their idea of school might have emanated from such policy discourse. In fact, by singling out individuals who never went to school as the legitimate actors and characters in the world of adult literacy learning, the primer implicitly suggests that the literacy classes are schools for adults. However, what was interesting to me was how these literacy learners went further to create actors and characters (Holland *et al*, 1998) with roles and acts that were in opposition to the official figured worlds of adult literacy learning. Their figuring confirmed that indeed 'figured worlds rest upon people's abilities to form and be formed in collectively realized "as if" realms' (ibid: 49). Through such abilities, the adult literacy learners refigured their literacy learning as being the same as primary schools. They argued that they learnt the same things as those taught in primary schools. The only difference they saw was that *'we are not flogged when we do something wrong'*.

The adult literacy learners' stance towards the authority of their instructors was reminiscent of my own experiences during my primary and secondary school days. As a pupil, my colleagues and I saw the teachers as all-knowing and therefore, their decisions could not be questioned. Discipline was about listening and doing what the teachers wanted us to do. This 'school culture' appeared to be the same as the one literacy learners and their instructors were enacting at this literacy centre.

Agency, improvisation and resistance in figured worlds

Although the adult literacy learners viewed themselves as *wali* (initiates, see Chapter 6) who had to be told what to do, sometimes they exercised agency and resistance. Thus, the potency of the 'school culture' was not unbounded. Citing Inden (1990), Holland *et al* (ibid: 42) describe human agency as

> the realized capacity of people to act upon their world and not only to know about or give personal or intersubjective significance to it. That capacity is the power of people to act purposively and reflectively, in more or less complex interrelationships with one another, to reiterate and remake the world in which they live, in circumstances where they may consider different courses of action possible and desirable, though not necessarily from the same point of view.

As illustrated in Chapter 6, the adult literacy learners sometimes resisted their instructor's demands to sing songs. They also employed their agency to defy their instructors' adherence to the stated English literacy enrolment policy in which only Chichewa literacy 'graduates' were to be allowed to participate in English lessons. This shows that indeed people are capable of reasserting 'a point of control through the rearrangement of cultural forms as evocations of position' (ibid: 45). In this case, the literacy learners argued that there was no link between their ability to read and write in Chichewa to learning English. They cited the learning of English by kids in kindergarten as their cultural means to counteract their instructors' English policy arguments. Consequently, some of them resisted the instructors' argument and exercised their agency to enrol for English literacy lessons.

Besides, the adult literacy learners resisted any decision the instructors made that clashed with their priorities. On several occasions, the instructors suggested that the number of days for holding literacy classes should be increased from three to at least four. However, the literacy learners resisted to have classes on Thursdays because it was one of the market days on which they ordered items for their businesses. They also resisted any proposal to hold literacy classes on Friday because this day was set aside for prayers. Moreover, when the planting season came, they suspended the literacy classes against their instructors' recommendations. The agency and resistance these literacy learners exercised in these instances demonstrated that 'even within grossly asymmetrical power relations, the powerful participants rarely control the weaker so completely that the latter's ability to improvise resistance becomes irrelevant' (Holland et al, 1998: 277). For these literacy learners, their agency and resistance afforded them the opportunities to accomplish what they desired most as individuals.

At the beginning of my fieldwork I often heard the instructor tell the literacy learners to be ready for examinations. In keeping with her plea, she sometimes gave the learners tests and on one such occasion, she complained about the literacy learners' performance saying:

but what disappointed me was that the whole class I had yesterday, I am not sure whether there were 13 or 14 literacy learners, when one literacy learner got one problem wrong everyone failed the same. I do not know how it happened. Tomorrow we are writing another test and I want everyone to sit on their own. I want to see each person's individual performance.

(Field notes: 25 November 2015)

Here the instructor appeared to suggest that the learners were sharing their work and that such acts were inappropriate. She was trying to encourage the learners to adhere to the norms and expectations of the official figuring of examinations. In such a context, independent writing was the act that had significance. She therefore gave them another test. The instructor's remarks and her emphasis on individual performance resonated with my own figuring of assessment as a teacher in a formal educational setting.

So, when the examination day came, I was keen to observe and learn how the learners played out their role as examination candidates. Sitting on a bench in the examination room I recalled my own experiences with exams both as a learner and as a teacher. I remembered how intimidated I felt each time I was sitting for an exam and wondered whether the literacy learners felt the same. When the exams started it was discovered that the exam scripts were inadequate and the learners were asked to copy the questions first. The instructor wanted to ensure that each learner answered the questions independently. However, this resource constraint provided an opportunity to the adult literacy learners to disrupt the cherished school norm of working out exam answers independently by improvising their own approach. Realizing that the situation they had was rather novel, the learners exercised their agency and grouped themselves together and began to write the exams disregarding their instructors' request. That improvisation disrupted not only the 'formal school norm' but also the figuring of examination such that collaborative efforts thrived alongside independent exam writing. The significance of what these learners did is that such improvisations could 'constitute the environment or landscape in which the experience of the next generation "sediments," falls out, into expectation and disposition' (Holland *et al*, 1998: 18).

Overall, the adult literacy learners' agency revealed the challenges of enforcing a strict bureaucratic operational system in an activity whose participants join voluntarily. Such an operational system created complex power relationships among the participants, putting some of them in perpetual dilemmas. As we saw in Chapter 6, despite understanding the plight of the women, the instructors could not act on the women's request to suspend the literacy classes because they were afraid that one of the official artefacts would expose them. In this case, it appeared as though the district officers' action had been taken over or was delegated to the artefacts (Latour, 2005). When the literacy learners finally exercised their agency and suspended the lessons, tensions were palpable amongst the instructors concerning who authorized it. As I understood it, the instructors' major concerns were not about the disruption the suspension was going to cause to literacy learning, rather it was about the implications it had on the security of their jobs.

In short, I would argue that the refiguring of the adult literacy learning as school narrowed the space within which the adult literacy learners could exercise power and agency, thereby limiting their role in decision-making processes. In Chapter 6, I looked at cases whereby the instructors gave the learners opportunities to state what they wanted to learn but the latter usually remained silent. The least they could do was to mention the difficulties they had with some arithmetic problems. Yet in some contexts, they were facing shame and humiliation due to their failure to read and write. In addition, they were receiving different kinds of artefacts they needed to read and understand. They could not mention any of these. In private, they told me what their interests were and they claimed that they did not tell the literacy instructors what they wanted to learn because '*we are afraid of the instructors*'. They saw the dominance of the instructors as a legitimate norm, that is, '*that is how things should be*'. The cases cited in this section demonstrate that 'human agency may be frail, especially among those with little power, but it happens daily and mundanely, and it deserves our attention' (ibid: 5).

Literacy learning and positioning in social change

Holland *et al* (1998) make us understand that every person views their lived worlds through the lenses of the positions they are 'persistently cast'. In Chapter 1, I noted that the Malawi Government perceives poverty, ignorance and disease as the enemies it should fight and defeat. I also observed that the government constructs literacy as a major tool for promoting the figured world of development. To enact this world, the government employs a cultural model that interactively positions non-literate people as individuals with deficits. That is, non-literate people are figured out as lacking the ability 'to understand and make use [of] many of the modern techniques, ideas and messages relating to improved living standards and values' (Ministry of Gender, Child Welfare and Community Services, 2005: 6). They are therefore expected to 'develop their abilities, [and] enrich their knowledge in order to change their attitudes and values' (ibid: 6).

This figuring appears to have been internalized by the literacy officers at the district office. As I illustrated in Chapter 7, the district literacy officers said that the learners' acquisition of reading and writing skills was not their primary concern. To them, the goal of the NALP in Malawi was to see some behavioural transformation amongst the literacy learners. By saying this, the officers interactively positioned the adult literacy learners as individuals whose behaviour was inappropriate.

This figuring is evident in some of the stories the adult literacy learners read and discussed from their primer. The stories were mostly written in the manner that denigrated the assumed local knowledge and practices which the literacy learners were perceived to possess and do, and glorified the 'new' ones which the programme assumed they lacked. The structure of the stories epitomized the assumptions the NALP made regarding the state of knowledge the literacy learners had, and the practices they were involved in, and concluded with what the programme expected them to be upon completion. At the same time, the stories typified how a figured world of social change was constructed and reified. Overall, both the structure of the said stories and the figuring of the world of social change were unidirectional and therefore provided the adult literacy learners with only one subject position, that is, *the not knowledgeable* (the ignorant).

However, in Chapter 5, I showed that some of the learners such as Ms Awali were not entirely oblivious of the issues discussed in the literacy classes. They said that most of the issues they were reading from the primer were not new to them. Ms Awali said that the learners took part in discussing such issues in class just because the instructors brought them up and they felt obliged to contribute.

Looking at the way the literacy officers at the district office talked about literacy and social change, I got the impression that they assumed that the process was somehow straightforward. That is, they appeared to think that once the adult literacy learners were 'enlightened', then they were going to amend their ways of doing things. On the contrary, my discussions in that chapter have shown that the application of the knowledge purported to have been gained from the literacy classes was far more complex than it was thought. I have shown that a number of factors such as trust, community members' tastes, as well as their personal fears influenced the use of such knowledge.

In Chapter 3, I indicated that Sawabu village had some basic facilities such as piped water. However, water and health experts considered this water unsafe for human consumption. As such, they encouraged community members to apply chlorine which was made available at each water tap as shown in Figure 17 below but some community members were reluctant to use it.

The villagers suspected that the chlorine was a chemical which the government wanted to use to stop them from bearing more children. Incidentally, birth control is one of the topics covered in the adult literacy primer. When the learners discussed this topic in class, they reflexively positioned themselves as individuals who already had knowledge of birth control. Some of them cautioned against the 'modern' methods of birth control. Ms Mkakosya narrated her personal story and questioned the effectiveness of some of the contraceptives she used. Others such as Ms Awali cited some complications or negative side effects their loved ones went through after using some of the contraceptives. Possibly, such experiences could explain their reluctance to be drawn into using chlorine which they suspected to be a form of birth control.

Apart from trust, the literacy learners' tastes mattered as well. The issue of making water safe for drinking was also discussed in one of the literacy lessons. The literacy learners talked about various ways of making water safe for drinking, including boiling and filtering it. However, some of them said that they did not

Figure 17 Blue Chlorine Dispenser

boil their drinking water because once it is boiled, the water loses its taste. As for chlorine, apart from the suspicion discussed earlier, the literacy learners said that they did not use it because they did not like its smell which they said made them feel sick.

Lastly, their quest to safeguard their marriages and self-image also influenced the decisions they made on whether to do what they learnt in class or not. For example, when they discussed gender roles during one of their lessons, the literacy learners said they would not allow their husbands to do a 'woman's' job such as pounding maize. They said that they would not even try it for fear of breaking their marriages. They argued that even if they did try and their husbands agreed to help in doing it, the community at large would accuse them of casting some spells on their husbands and that their husbands would be subjected to ridicule. For them, the husbands were the heads of their families and they could not therefore be subjected to doing what they considered to be a 'woman's' job. Thus, the literacy learners were very much interested in reflexively positioning themselves as 'good wives' in the eyes of the community at large. They employed their assumed cultural expectations as their 'prescriptive norms' (Heath & Street, 2008) to justify their perceptions. Thus, the issue was more than just lack of knowledge. The women were looking at a bigger picture than the simplistic approach the literacy lessons were propagating. In this case it was not just about the women changing but rather the entire society.

Also, the learners' perspectives of social change were linked to developments taking place in broader social contexts. In Chapter 4, I noted that although mediation offered the women the means to navigate through tasks that required literacy, some of them resented the practice because they said people were no longer trustworthy. Furthermore, the women were aware that the new developments in the education sector such as the provision of free primary school had changed the way the community perceived non-literate individuals, especially those presumed to be young. They noted how reluctant officers were to help such individuals in literacy practices based on the assumption that they chose to be non-literate. These developments formed the basis for the literacies they sought.

What comes out from the foregoing discussion is a disjuncture between what the literacy providers assume the literacy lessons would achieve and what was happening in practice. There was a contrast between the powerful official discourses that interactively constructed and positioned the adult literacy learners as passive and lacking agency on the one hand, and the literacy learners' discourses that reflexively positioned them as receptive but constrained by cultural traditions and expectations on the other. It should be noted however, that my intention in acknowledging these cultural traditions is not to essentialize them, but rather to highlight 'what culture does' (Street, 2010: 581) to these literacy learners. In this case, culture appeared to 'define and name' (ibid) the practices of a good wife. Besides, the discussion also raises the issue of power imbued in literacy learning. In a nutshell, it can be said that although the programme's construction of social change succeeds in positioning the learners as *the not knowledgeable* and therefore, to some extent, 'wrong doers', it falls short of assessing and understanding why they do some of the things it seeks to change. The programme does not consider that some of the adult literacy learners' actions were based on, for instance, their knowledge about family planning including their beliefs as well as experiences regarding the smell or taste of treated water. Besides, the conformist approach to social change advocated by the NALP in Malawi is rather limited since it does not provide any room to the individuals it recruits and assumes require 'enlightenment' to reflect on and change their social practices. Overall this demonstrates the ineffectiveness of enforcing change without a proper understanding of the context.

Authoring and re-authoring identities in figured worlds

Generally, community members at Sawabu village assumed that anyone who was not able to read and write did not go to school. Hence the dominant subject positions they assigned themselves or others were *the educated, the uneducated, the intelligent and the unintelligent* (see Chapter 5).

The literacy practices promoted in adult literacy learning made Ms Msosa interactively position Ms Mkakosya, Ms Afiki, Ms Balala, Ms Abasi, as *the educated*. Her reason for doing so was that whenever the instructors asked these literacy learners to either read or write, they were able to do so without any assistance. So, Ms Msosa used her knowledge of the literacy practices valued in the adult literacy class as her cultural resources to ascribe the four women an identity of being *the educated* (the able to read and write). On her part, Ms Msosa had some difficulties in participating adequately in the literacy activities privileged in adult literacy learning. She faced challenges in writing words on the chalkboard as well as reading the stories from the primer in the literacy class. Consequently, she reflexively positioned herself as *the uneducated*. Thus, the practices the adult literacy learners performed in class, allowed Ms Msosa 'to recognize' each one of the four women above 'as a particular sort of actor' (Urrieta Jr., 2007).

Nonetheless, when I interviewed her at her home, Ms Msosa appeared to negotiate her *uneducated* identity by using the resources at her disposal and re-authored herself to become *the educated*. She showed me a book she kept in her house. As I flipped through the pages of the book, she read the contents of the pages. Thus, through this *socially situated activity* (reading in my presence), Ms Msosa appeared to enact a *socially situated identity* (Gee, 2005) leading me to recognize her as someone who was able to read (*the educated*). Certainly, this shows that 'none of us is occupied singularly: we are not possessed by one identity, one discourse, one subject position' (Holland *et al*, 1998: 211). Ms Msosa's case also suggested that instead of empowering her, the literacy practices that were promoted in the literacy class disempowered her. Since the adult literacy learners treated me as one of the literacy officers (see Chapter 3), by 'reading' from her book in my presence, Ms Msosa demonstrated to me, consciously or otherwise, that although my colleagues and I interactively positioned her as *the uneducated*, we were somehow imposing (Gee, 2000–2001) this identity on her. That is, she implicitly rejected the identity that the instructors and I somewhat ascribed to her. Hence, just as she used the literacy practices and the artefacts employed in the literacy class to 'affect others' she used her own artefact to affect herself (Holland *et al*, 1998).

Ms Msosa was not the only literacy learner who employed the cultural resources associated with school to author her own and other literacy learners' subject positions. Ms Kalako did the same. Ms Kalako had problems coping with the literacy activities privileged in the literacy class. This was evident when the instructors asked her to write words on the chalkboard. The instructors dictated the letters to her. She wrote them down but when they asked her to combine and read them as words, she could not. Meanwhile, Ms Kalako was aware that the instructors were interactively positioning some adult literacy learners such as Ms Mkakosya, Ms Afiki, Ms Balala and Ms Tepani as the *intelligent* ones because of their ability to read and write. Hence, during an interview with me, she reflexively assigned herself the 'natural identity' (Gee, 2000–2001) of being *unintelligent*.[1] That is, she linked her perceived struggles with literacy in the literacy class with her assumed naturally limited intellectual endowment and employed them as her cultural resources to author her subject position.

Interestingly, some of the adult literacy learners who were interactively positioned as *the educated* and *the intelligent* sometimes employed their literacy and numeracy knowledge as tools for re-authoring themselves (Holland *et al*, 1998) and reflexively positioned themselves as instructors. In Chapter 5, I illustrated how Ms Balala and Ms Imani insisted that the supervisor should explain to the 'other' literacy learners the value of 1 (one) borrowed from another number during subtraction. When he resisted offering the explanation they demanded, they asked him: '*so, have you failed to answer the question Sir?*' They then offered to do the explanation, thereby reflexively positioning themselves as *the instructors*. They emphasized the fact that the explanation they were seeking was for the benefit of the other literacy learners and not them, saying, '*they must know that the 1 (one) has the value of 10*'. By saying this, the two literacy learners re-authored their identity and repositioned themselves relative to their colleagues. They implicitly made it known that although the literacy class ascribed them the identity of being *the not knowledgeable*, they had something to offer. Their insistence in this matter somehow disrupted the 'school culture' I discussed in Chapter 6 and these disruptions showed that indeed

> when individuals learn about figured worlds and come, in some sense, to identify themselves in those worlds, their participation may include reactions to the treatment they have received as occupants of the positions figured by the worlds.
>
> (ibid: 45)

---

[1] In Ciyawo, Ms Kalako said 'ligongo jwangali lunda' which could literally be rendered as 'because I do not have intelligence; i.e. because I am not intelligent'.

However, such re-authoring is expected because positional identities (ibid) are never stable. In this case, the literacy learners used the same knowledge that put the supervisor in a position of authority to disrupt the 'school culture' and somehow resist their identities. The supervisor understood this disruption and attempted to reassert his authority, saying: '*But let us leave this aside. It can confuse you. Is that understood? Am I right, Ms Balala?*' By telling Ms Balala not to pursue the issue any further to avoid being confused, the supervisor was not only claiming his position as the legitimate source of knowledge but also as the gatekeeper of the same. The supervisor positioned himself as the authority who cared and knew what was good for the adult literacy learners. The two closed questions which he asked were meant to stamp his authority and force the two literacy learners into submission, thereby taking up their 'legitimate' subordinate subject position assigned to them by the adult literacy class.

The adult literacy learners' self-authoring (ibid) was very much pronounced when a stand-in instructor from a nearby dysfunctional literacy centre facilitated the literacy lessons. They kept on correcting both her writing and reading and sometimes the tension in the classroom was palpable as I witnessed in the following exchange.

Ms Balala: Madam, could you write that 'r' properly, it looks like a seven (7)
Stand-in instructor: This 'r?' Does 7 face this way (pointing to the right)? I thought it faces that way (pointing to the left).
Ms Balala: Just write it for us.

What we see here is an attempt by the instructor to stamp her authority by using her knowledge of the letters and numbers but Ms Balala resisted it. Ms Balala's final utterance is an imperative statement and not a request. As such, the instructor had to do it whether she liked it or not. Hence the instructor's explanation was not relevant. What was required of her was to write properly the disputed letter. It was situations like this that made some of the adult literacy learners who were positioned as *the educated* and *the intelligent* reflexively position themselves as *instructors*, arguing that they could teach better than she did. At the same time, these literacy learners appeared to position this instructor as *the incompetent* one. Somewhat, the instructor appeared to have sensed this, hence her attempt to resist that subject position.

These discussions show that the adult literacy class provided the space in which the learners' and the instructors' 'social positions and social relationships [were] named and conducted' (Holland *et al*, 1998: 60). The literacy practices promoted in this context provided the means through which the adult literacy learners constructed their literacy self-image relative to others. While some adult literacy learners internalized and accepted their 'institutional identities' (Gee, 2000–2001), others sometimes re-authored and repositioned themselves subject to the context, thereby demonstrating that an individual's identities can never be settled once and for all.

Artefacts and identities in figured worlds

The activities in which some community members in Sawabu village participated employed various artefacts which required specific practices (see Chapter 4). These artefacts such as the ration card in emergency food assistance, and the money card in the Social Cash Transfer programmes enabled the beneficiaries to participate in these initiatives. To some extent, these documents evoked these initiatives as the lived worlds of the community members who were recruited into them. For instance, the ration card appeared to evoke a world of community members who were believed to be victims of natural disasters, that is, 'people affected by shocks'. In this world, only those community members rendered food-insecure by natural disasters were recognized as beneficiaries; free food distribution was the only act valued and the ration card was the only acceptable artefact. In this regard, the card was not just a piece of paper. It had some value. Besides, it made some community members stand out as the most food-insecure in the area.

In this section, I focus on two artefacts which the villagers encountered in official figured worlds namely, the pen and the inkpad because of two reasons. First, the two artefacts appeared to serve across the community members' lived worlds, especially where one was required to put a mark of one type or the other as evidence of their participation. Second, and more importantly, the two artefacts appeared to arouse polarized emotions from community members who used them.

Listening to some community members talk about their experiences in certain literacy practices, there was a sense that pens and inkpads were not just tools one used to acknowledge receipt of either food aid or cash. These artefacts appeared to symbolize different worlds to which some community members either claimed or were denied membership. The pen evoked the world of the literate. Hence, holding a pen was not just a physical act but also a declaration that one was literate because 'cultural artefacts are essential for identity work' (Bartlett, 2005: 3) In this case, by getting hold of the pen, community members such as Ms Awali consciously or unconsciously made a claim about their literacy identity. Though interactively positioned as non-literate in the literacy class, by getting hold of the pen, a valued cultural artefact for literacy, Ms Awali negotiated her identity and repositioned herself as someone who was literate. This shows that undeniably 'one way in which people develop the figured elements of their identities and thus counteract powerful social positioning is through the adoption and use of powerful, compelling cultural resources, or artefacts' (ibid). Ms Awali appeared to have succeeded in counteracting such powerful social positioning as evidenced by the response she got from the officers, that is, *'we respect you'*. This shows that '[artefacts] are not inert beings but have real effects when they are activated through networks' (Hamilton, 2016: 8).

While the pen symbolized literacy and somehow afforded pride and respect to those who could *'get hold of it'*, the inkpad symbolized 'illiteracy', thereby making those who pressed their thumbs on it as a way of signing feel shame and humiliation. This state of affairs was exacerbated by the fact that, although the latter provided non-literate community members opportunities to participate in activities that required writing, some officers had negative attitudes towards it. For example, Ms Afiki, one of the adult literacy learners, complained in class that community members who were not able to read and write were looked down upon during the distribution of free mosquito nets. And when the supervisor asked as to whether the officers had ink or not, she said: *'they had it but they looked at you contemptuously'*. As for some of the women who actually used the inkpad during such occasions, their feeling of shame and humiliation was profound, as I found out from Ms Faki.

> *Sometimes I print using my thumb but I feel ashamed. Others are using a pen to sign their names and I am using a thumb print, it is shameful. As you leave you feel like the earth is going to open up and swallow you up. Now I am slowly learning how to write my name.*
>
> (Field notes: 28 May 2016)

Here, the contrast between the feelings emanating from the use of the two artefacts came out very clearly to me. While one could walk with their head up after using a pen, the other felt like the world was crumbling under their feet after using the inkpad. When I tried to find out from Ms Suwedi why she thought some officers did not like thumb printing, she told me that the officers said that *'when you print using your thumb, you spoil their forms because the ink spills over on to the lines others were supposed to sign in'.*

However, not all community members appeared to be ashamed of thumb printing, that is, the inkpad. Some saw it as a norm. During an FGD, Ms Suya said:

> *this is what we have been doing all these years. When they call us, they know that we are old. So, they grab our hands and make us print using our thumbs. Sometimes those who attend literacy classes write things that are not legible and the officials say, 'you have not written anything meaningful here. Just print using your thumb.' Which one is more shameful than the other, to just go and print using your thumb straight away or to be told to print using your thumb after being stopped from signing?*
>
> (Field notes: 18 June 2016)

In this extract, Ms Suya appeared to suggest that the pen did not always afford respect to those who used it. Rather the respect was earned through competence. As Ms Suya put it, an unsuccessful attempt at using the pen brought with it damaging consequences. But although Ms Suya said that she did not have any problems with thumb printing, it appeared that she was just being pragmatic because as the discussion continued, she said:

> *we can go and enrol for adult literacy classes. But for us to be able to write is something I do not believe that it is possible. Our hands are a bit feeble. I do not think that we can handle the pen.*
>
> (Field notes: 18 June 2016)

Here Ms Suya appeared to suggest that the pen was best suited for the relatively young community members as opposed to the individuals considered to be old whose hands were *feeble*. To some extent, Ms Suya implied that she did not have any other option than using the inkpad due to her perceived old age. One may argue, therefore, that the way the two items were being utilized by some of the community members shows that artefacts are 'tools that people use to affect their own and others' thinking, feeling, and behaviour' (Holland *et al*, 1998: 50).

I should quickly point out though that the issue of thumb printing and shame was more complex than it appeared at face value. First, it had something to do with one's status in society. This was the case with Ms Duniya. As I stated in Chapter 4, Ms Duniya was a traditional leader in her community. As someone who was highly respected in her community, the act of thumb printing posed a threat to her social standing relative to her subjects. By virtue of her position, Ms Duniya was involved in many literacy practices both at home and in government- and NGO-organized activities elsewhere. While she always got some help from her counsellors and niece to navigate through literacy-mediated activities at home, she sometimes had to hunt for helpers in other contexts which she said was humiliating. She recounted an occasion in which officers ridiculed her because she had to use the inkpad and she felt disgraced.

Second, the age of the person involved also sometimes mattered. Most of the literacy learners who narrated shameful experiences with thumb printing were relatively young. These literacy learners said they were laughed and shouted at. Above all, they were denigrated when they printed using their thumbs. They talked about the responsible officers wondering as to why they had not taken advantage of the country's free primary education which the Malawi government introduced in 1994. They recounted instances in which as they printed using their thumbs, they were sarcastically asked: *'where were you?'* In some way, this question implied that the women who used their thumbs to print were somehow irresponsible. That is, they were being questioned as to where they were when others were in school as if all of them chose to be out of school. They said that they were told to enrol for the adult literacy lessons. It was encounters like these that made them feel ashamed. At the same time, community members who were assumed to be old such as Ms Suya and her sisters were treated somewhat respectfully. The officers were ready to help them print using their thumbs, hence, *'they grab our hands and make us print using our thumbs'*. Ms Suya said that she was used to this practice. To some extent, this explains why the officers were surprised when they saw that Ms Awali, who they considered to be old, was ready to sign her name.

Third, shame was instigated by the attitudes some officers had towards thumb printing. Ms Suwedi enrolled for the literacy lessons to learn how to write her name because she had an encounter with some officers who insisted that she should sign her name. They wrote her name on a piece of paper and made her copy it onto their forms. She was told that they did not want their forms to be spoilt through thumb printing. Ms Balala talked about some officers who sometimes publicly announced that thumb printing would not be allowed, *'everyone must sign their name'*. Such tendencies did not go unnoticed. Some community members such as Ms Kalako could not hide their displeasure concerning the demand for one to sign their name. She recollected that *'in the past thumb printing was not an issue but these days things have gone bad'*.

The discussion in this section shows that artefacts are not inert objects in figured worlds. The use of either of these two items implied a claim of subject position which some community members either cherished or denigrated.

Holland and Cole (1995) use a hammer as an example to explain what artefacts do, saying 'every hammer can be seen as an encapsulated "theory of the task" and simultaneously a "theory of the person" who fulfils the task' (p. 482). Similarly, the pen and the inkpad were not just 'theories' of the tasks to which they were employed but also of the individuals who employed them. It was not what these artefacts allowed the women to do that mattered most, rather it was what they did to the women that was significant.

Implications for literacy theory

In Chapter 2, I stated that my work was grounded on the notion that literacy is a social practice. I also noted that some literacy theorists and experts tend to share the view that literacy is intertwined with power and identity (see Street, 1993; Collins & Blot, 2003; Papen, 2005; St. Clair, 2010). However, my critical review of literature on the social theory of literacy revealed that there were certain aspects of literacy, particularly those concerning power relations and identity, I could not examine adequately if I confined my work exclusively to this theory. The key challenge was that although through the ideological model, the social theory of literacy recognizes power and identity, it does less in providing conceptual tools with which to analyse and understand these aspects in literacy practices. I therefore decided to integrate it with Holland *et al*'s (1998) sociocultural theory of self and identity, especially the concept of figured world. From Holland *et al*'s theory, I identified a number of conceptual tools such as positioning, cultural means, artefacts and agency which I complemented with Gee's (1999) conceptualization of identities as well as Davies and Harré's (2007) ideas of interactive and reflexive positioning.

The discussions in the preceding chapters attest the complex interplay between literacy, power and identity. They have revealed that just as literacy varied from one context to another, the same was true with literacy identities, subject to what the actors and characters in the specific figured worlds valued. Besides, they have also established that while the more powerful actors ascribed literacy identities to the less powerful participants in some contexts, the latter sometimes resisted, negotiated or refigured and performed the literacy identities they desired. What these discussions suggest, therefore, is that studying literacy in relation to power and identity adds to our understanding of the multiplicity of literacies including the complexity and fluidity of being literate or non-literate. Crucially, the discussions suggest that the concept of figured world has the potential of enhancing literacy studies based on the social theory of literacy in a Malawian context.

Implications for policy and practice

This book is based on my interactions with some community members in a small village in Malawi. Therefore, it would be problematic to draw on these interactions and generalize about the National Adult Literacy Programme or indeed literacy practices in other parts of the country. The value of my ethnographic account lies, in part, in the potential it has in offering 'an element of critical reflection' (Mosse, 2004: 667) towards policy processes.

My discussions in Chapter 5 revealed that some adult literacy learners felt disenfranchised in classroom literacy practices because they were put together with other literacy learners who already knew how to read and write. At the same time, I have illustrated that the adult literacy learners enrolled for the literacy lessons with different expectations. These cases imply that the NALP needs to consider providing some space for other literacies to be taught at this literacy class instead of privileging just one. Paradoxically, my examples have also revealed that to some extent, the school culture which the same literacy learners enacted at this literacy centre constrained them to articulate such expectations. What this suggests is that there is need to find ways of balancing between respecting their conscious or unconscious refiguring of their literacy learning as a formal class on the one hand, and meeting their expectations on the other, that is, there is need to explore not only the 'instrumental uses of literacy' but also 'examine the symbolic roles literacy and education play in people's lives' (Papen, 2005: 14).

My discussions have also established how a top-down approach to policy formulation and implementation sometimes created tensions among participants at this centre. I have illustrated how some women were denied the opportunity to join the English literacy classes because of an English literacy policy which some adult literacy learners questioned and defied. Given the 'school culture' I referred to in Chapter 6, the 'self-promotion' which some adult literacy learners effected to join the English literacy class was not appreciated by their instructors. Based on these examples, I would therefore suggest that there is a need for greater flexibility in the operations of this literacy centre, especially when it comes to responding to adult literacy learners' wishes because the 'governance brought by [those in authority] cannot be imposed; it requires collaboration and compromise' (Mosse, 2005: 7).

Implications for language use in a multilingual literacy classroom

The discussion in Chapter 7 has revealed the complexities surrounding the issue of language of instruction in a multilingual adult literacy classroom. The situation is made even more complicated by the fact that the learners are exposed to multiple literacies both inside their literacy class as well as in the lived worlds. This implies that the decision regarding which language(s) should be used in an adult literacy classroom in this context may not be guided by pedagogical concerns alone. I have illustrated the contradictory consequences of using either the national language, Chichewa or mother tongue in this setting. As an official language, the use of Chichewa in the classroom appeared to empower the women to gain access to dominant literacies. At the same time the language alienated other learners just as Dulani and Chinsinga (2006) had reported. Similarly, I have demonstrated that although the use of mother tongues may facilitate easy learning of some literacies and also enhance the learners' linguistic identities, this practice may also impede the acquisition of the linguistic capital the learners would require in official figured worlds.

Robinson-Pant (2001) reports similar language use issues in literacy programmes in Nepal. Based on such challenges and writing within the context of literacy and development, Robinson-Pant argues (ibid) that 'planners need to explore more about how certain literacies and languages are identified with different kinds of development by women of varying backgrounds' (p. 74). She concludes by saying that 'language policy can then reflect ideological as well as technical or functional concerns' (ibid). To some extent, this means avoiding the imposition of a 'single orthodoxy' (McCaffery, Merrifield & Millican, 2007) in dealing with these matters. It suggests offering 'enough flexibility to respond to the particular (and changing) needs and interests of participants and communities, and how they want to use literacy, and take them beyond the things they know' (ibid: 260).

Implications for literacy research methodology

The study on which this book is based explored community members' literacy practices, discourses, meanings, identities, as well as power relations in their lived worlds. My decision to conduct it through an ethnographic approach was informed by my belief that 'as a set of methods, ethnography is not far removed from the means that we all use in everyday life to make sense of our surroundings, of other people's actions, and perhaps even of what we do ourselves' (Hammersley & Atkinson, 2007: 4). By using more than one method to examine and understand a specific literacy phenomenon, the reliability of my data was, to some extent, tested. For instance, while observing the literacy lessons I often heard both the literacy learners and the instructors identify some individuals as *not knowing anything*. I picked up this figuring in informal conversations with instructors who explained to me what *not knowing anything* meant to her (see Chapter 5). I also picked up the same during semi-structured interviews with some of those adult literacy learners who were assumed not to know anything before enrolling for the literacy lessons, such as Ms Kalako, Ms Suwedi and Ms Maulidi. In so doing, I was able to deepen my understanding of this discourse from multiple perspectives.

Although this approach offered me an opportunity to provide 'thick descriptions' (Geertz, 1973) of people's practices of everyday life, there were some unexpected lessons I learnt. First, much as I tried to integrate myself and be part of the community, to some community members, I remained a stranger. This was exacerbated by my institutional identity (Gee, 2000–2001) of being a university teacher. Being someone who was more educated academically, I was given the title of headmaster by the community members. On several occasions, I was asked to provide guidance on how the classes should be organized although I tried to avoid being involved in such matters. This suggests that my presence in this community reinforced the 'school culture' the community members were enacting at the adult literacy class.

Second, although being a native speaker of the language predominantly spoken in the community and a member of the religion practised by most of the community members played a part in making some community members cautiously take me as their own, sometimes it created some dilemmas. For instance, on several occasions, the supervisor and the resident instructors, who were non-Muslims, suggested holding literacy classes on Fridays. During informal conversations, some literacy learners 'tactfully' sought my opinion on such sensitive matters not just as their 'headmaster' but also as a member of their faith. Distancing myself from such decisions would result in having the literacy officers construed as being insensitive to the learners' faith. Accepting my involvement in the same would raise questions regarding my faith. The least I did was to ask them to explain to me how and who was responsible for making such decisions. What this implies is that belonging to the same category as the research participants may sometimes have some costs. Therefore, one has to tread carefully.

Third, in line with the tenets of an ethnographic approach, I tried as much as I could to spend most of my time in the community. Paradoxically, I realized that living in the community was not enough for me to gain access to some community members' everyday literacy practices. For example, the community members who took part in relief and related programme activities kept the dates and venues to themselves. I only saw them on their way back carrying whatever they had been given. Even my landlady, whose house was a few metres from my own, did not divulge details regarding when and where such activities would be conducted. In a context where many community members were aggrieved at their exclusion from the programmes concerned, I understood why such information was somehow sensitive. What this implies is that 'being there' was not equivalent to seeing everything. Under such circumstances, what I managed to do was to request those involved to share with me their experiences, especially with literacy in such activities.

Notwithstanding these challenges, participant observation allowed me to experience what both the literacy learners and their instructors were going through during the literacy lessons. Such interactions made me continuously question my assumptions and beliefs about literacy teaching and learning. I studied literacy in my earlier works but I found this study rewarding because it was not just about understanding my participants, but it was also about learning about myself. The opportunities I was given to facilitate some literacy lessons made me understand what it means to teach adults. These encounters made me realize that apart from educational qualifications, you need a heart to teach adults.

References

Agar, M. H. (1996). *The Professional Stranger*. (2nd Ed.). San Diego: Academic Press.
Anderson, B. (1991). *Imagined Communities*. (Revised Ed.). London: Verso.
Atkinson P. and Hammersley, M. (1994). Ethnography and Participant Observation. In N. K. Denzin and Y. S. Lincoln (Eds.). *Handbook of Qualitative Research*. Thousand Oaks: SAGE Publications.
Bandura, A. (1971). *Social Learning Theory*. New York: General Learning Press.
Bartlett, L. (2005). Identity Work and Cultural Artefacts in Literacy Learning and Use: A Sociocultural Analysis. *Language and Education*, 19, 1.
Bartlett, L. (2007). Literacy, Speech and Shame: the Cultural Politics of Literacy and Language in Brazil. *International Journal of Qualitative Studies in Education*, 20, 5, 547–63.
Bartlett, L. (2008a). To Seem and to Feel: Engaging Cultural Artefacts to 'Do' Literacy. In M. Prinsloo and M. Baynham (Eds.). *Literacies, Global and Local*. Amsterdam: John Benjamins Publishing Company.
Bartlett, L. (2008b). Literacy's Verb: Exploring What Literacy is and What Literacy Does. *International Journal of Educational Development*, 28, 737–53. DOI: 10.1016/j.ijedudev.2007.09.002.
Bartlett, L. (2010). *The Word and the World: The Cultural Politics of Literacy in Brazil*. New Jersey: Hampton Press Inc.
Bartlett, L. and Holland, D. (2002). *Theorising the Space of Literacy Practices*. Accessed on 28/1/17 from https://www.researchgate.net/publication/238355394
Barton, D. (2007). *Literacy: An Introduction to the Ecology of Written Language*. (2nd Ed.). Oxford: Blackwell Publishing.
Barton, D. (2009). Understanding Textual Practices in a Changing World. In M. Baynham and M. Prinsloo (Eds.). *The Future of Literacy Studies*. New York: Palgrave Macmillan.
Barton, D. and Hamilton, M. (1998). *Local Literacies: Reading and Writing in One Community*. London and New York: Routledge.
Barton, D. and Hamilton, M. (2000). Literacy Practices. In D. Barton, M. Hamilton and R. Ivanič (Eds.). *Situated Literacies: Reading and Writing in Context*. London and New York: Routledge.
Barton, D. and Hamilton, M. (2005). Literacy, Reification and the Dynamics of Social Interaction. In D. Barton and K. Tusting (Eds.). *Beyond Communities of Practice: Language Power and Social Context*. Cambridge: Cambridge University Press.
Barton, D., Hamilton, M. and Ivanič, R. (2000). Introduction: Exploring Situated Literacies. In D. Barton, M. Hamilton and R. Ivanič (Eds.). *Situated Literacies: Reading and Writing in Context*. London and New York: Routledge.

Barton, D. and Ivanič, R. (1991). (Eds.). *Writing in the Community*. London: Sage.

Barton, D. and Papen, U. (2010). (Eds.). *The Anthropology of Writing: Understanding Textually Mediated Worlds*. London: Continuum International Publishing Group.

Baynham, M. (1995). *Literacy Practices*. London and New York: Longman.

Baynham, M. and Prinsloo, M. (2009). The Future of Literacy Studies. In M. Baynham and M. Prinsloo (Eds.). *The Future of Literacy Studies*. New York: Palgrave Macmillan.

Becker, H. S. (1982). Culture: A Sociological View. *Yale Review*, 71, 513–27.

Benediktsson, K. and Kamtengeni, L. (2004). *Support to National Adult Literacy Programme 2001-2004: External Evaluation*. Lilongwe: ICEIDA.

Berge, E., Kambewa, D., Munthali, A. and Wiig, H. (2014). Lineage and Land Reforms in Malawi: Do Matrilineal and Patrilineal Landholdings Systems Represent a Problem in Land Reforms in Malawi? *Land Use Policy*, 41, 61–9.

Bhola, H. S. and Gómez, S. V. (2008). *Signposts to Literacy for Sustainable Development*. Hamburg: UNESCO Institute for Lifelong Learning.

Blommaert, J. (2004). Writing as a Problem: African Grassroots Writing, Economies of Literacy, and Globalization. *Language in Society*, 33, 643–71.

Blommaert, J. (2005). *Discourse: A Critical Introduction*. Cambridge: Cambridge University Press.

Bourdieu, P. (1977). The Economics of Linguistic Exchanges. *Social Science Information*, 16, 6, 645–68.

Brandt, D. and Clinton, K. (2002). Practice Limits of the Local: Expanding Perspectives on Literacy as a Social. *Journal of Literacy Research*, 34, 3, 337–56. DOI: 10.1207/s15548430jlr3403_4.

Braun, V. and Clarke, V. (2013). *Successful Qualitative Research: A Practical Guide for Beginners*. Los Angeles: SAGE Publications Ltd.

Bryman, A. (2008). *Social Research Methods*. (3rd Ed.). Oxford: Oxford University Press.

Bryman, A. (2012). *Social Research Methods*. (4th Ed.). Oxford: Oxford University Press.

Burns, B. B. (2000). *Introduction to Research Methods*. London: SAGE Publications.

Castles, S. (2015). International Human Mobility: Key Issues and Challenges to Social Theory. In Castles, S., Ozkul, D. and Cubas, M. A. (Eds.). *Social Transformation and Migration: National and Local Experiences in South Korea, Turkey, Mexico and Australia*. Hampshire: Palgrave.

Center for Social Research (2000). *Adolescent Girls' Literacy Project: Mid-term Evaluation Report*. Zomba; Malawi: Center for Social Research.

Chao, X. and Kuntz, A. (2013). Church-based ESL Program as a Figured World: Immigrant Adult Learners, Language, Identity, Power. *Linguistics and Education*, 24, 466–78.

Cheffy, I. P. (2008). *Conceptions of Literacy in Context Situated Understandings in a Rural Area of Northern Cameroon*. (PhD Thesis). University of Lancaster.

Chimombo, J. Chiuye G. (2002). 'Adult Basic and Literacy Education in Malawi: Provision and Delivery.' Paper presented at the International Conference on Adult

Basic and Literacy Education in the SADC Region at the University of Natal, South Africa. 3 to 5 November, 2002.

Chinsinga, B. (2006). The Interface between Tradition and Modernity: The Struggle for Political Space at the Local Level in Malawi. *Civilisations*, LIV, 1–2, 255–74. DOI: 10.4000/civilisations.498 URL: http://civilisations.revues.org/498.

Chinsinga, B. and Dulani, B. (2006). *Adult Literacy in Contemporary Malawi: What are the Issues?* Lilongwe: Ministry of Gender, Child Welfare and Community Services.

Chopra, P. (2008). *Parody and Power in the Gaze: (Re)presentations of the 'Illiterate Indian Village Woman'*. (PhD Thesis). London: Kings College.

Clifford, J. (1986). Introduction: Partial Truths. In J. Clifford and G. E. Marcus (Eds.). *Writing Culture: The Poetics and Politics of Ethnography*. Berkeley: University of California Press.

Cohen, L., Manion, L. and Morrison, K. (2007). *Research Methods in Education*. New York: Routledge.

Collins, J. and Blot, R. K. (2003). *Literacy and Literacies: Texts, Power and Identity*. Cambridge: Cambridge University Press.

Cooper, R. L. (1989). *Language Planning and Social Change*. Cambridge: Cambridge University Press.

Creswell, J.W. (2014). *Educational Research: Planning, Conducting and Evaluating Quantitative and Qualitative Research*. (4th Ed.). Essex: Pearson Education Ltd.

Crush, J. (1995). Introduction: Imagining Development. In J. Crush (Ed.). *Power of Development*. London: Routledge.

Dagenais, D., Day, E. and Toohey, K. (2006). A Multilingual Child's Literacy Practices and Contrasting Identities in the Figured Worlds of French Immersion Classrooms. *The International Journal of Bilingual Education and Bilingualism*, 9, 2, 205–18. DOI: 10.1080/13670050608668641.

Davies, B. and Harré, R. (2007). Positioning: The Discursive Production of Self. *Journal for the Theory of Social Behaviour*, 20, 1, 43–63. DOI:10.1111/j.1468-5914.1990.tb00174.

Delanty, G. (2003). *Community*. London and New York: Routledge.

Doronila, M. L. (1996). *Landscapes of Literacy*, Hamburg: UNESCO Institute for Education.

Escobar, A. (1995). *Encountering Development: The Making and Unmaking of the Third World*. Princeton: Princeton University Press.

Fairclough, N. (2001). *Language and Power*. (2nd Ed.). Harlow: Pearson Education Limited.

Food and Agriculture Organisation (2014). *Qualitative Research and Analyses of the Economic Impacts of Cash Transfers Programmes in Sub-Saharan Africa: Malawi Country Case Study*. Rome: FAO.

Freire, P. (1970). *Pedagogy of the Oppressed* (30th Anniversary Ed.). New York: The Continuum International Publishing Group Ltd.

Gebre, A.H., Rogers, A., Street, B. and Openjuru, G. (2009). *Everyday Literacies in Africa: Ethnographic Studies of Literacy and Numeracy Practices in Ethiopia*. Kampala: Fountain Publishers.

Gee, J. P. (1987). What Is Literacy? *Teaching and Learning*, 2, 1, 1–11.

Gee, J. P. (1999). *An Introduction to Discourse Analysis: Theory and Method*. London and New York: Routledge.

Gee, J. P. (2000–2001). Identity as an Analytic Lens for Research in Education. *Review of Research in Education*, 25, 99–125.

Gee, J. P. (2005). *An Introduction to Discourse Analysis: Theory and Method*. (2nd Ed.). London and New York: Routledge.

Gee, J. P. (2009). *A Situated Sociocultural Approach to Literacy and Technology*. Accessed on 19/1/17 from http://www.csun.edu/sites/default/files/James-Gee-sociotech.pdf

Gee, J. P. (2011). *An Introduction to Discourse Analysis: Theory and Method*. (3rd Ed.). London and New York: Routledge.

Geertz, C. (1973). *The Interpretation of Cultures: Selected Essays by Clifford Geertz*. New York: Basic Books Inc. Publishers.

Gereluk, D. (2006). *Education and Community*. London: Continuum.

Goody, J. and Watt, I. (1968). The Consequences of Literacy. In J. Goody (Ed.). *Literacy in Traditional Societies*. Cambridge: Cambridge University Press.

Government of Malawi (2011). *Implementation of Education Sector Millenium (sic) Development Goals (MDGs) and Education for All (EFA) Goals in Malawi*. Lilongwe: Ministry of Education.

Graff, H. J. (1979). *The Literacy Myth: Literacy and Social Structure in the 19th Century City, New York*. New York: Academic Press.

Guzzini, S. (2007). *Re-reading, or: The Three Fields for the Analysis of Power in International Relations*. Copenhagen: Danish Institute for International Studies.

Hamilton, M. (2000). Expanding the New Literacy Studies: Using Photographs to Explore Literacy as a Social Practice. In D. Barton, M. Hamilton and R. Ivanič (Eds.). *Situated Literacies: Reading and Writing in Context*. London and New York: Routledge.

Hamilton, M. (2012). *Literacy and the Politics of Representation*. New York: Routledge.

Hamilton, M. (2016). Imagining Literacy: A Sociomaterial Approach. In K. Yasukawa and S.Black (Eds.). *Beyond Economic Interests: Critical Perspectives on Adult Literacy and Numeracy in a Globalised World*. Rotterdam: Sense Publishers.

Hamilton, M. and Barton, D. and Ivanic, R. (Eds.). (1994). *Worlds of Literacy*. Clevedon, Avon: Multilingual Matters.

Hammersley, M. and Atkinson, P. (2007). *Ethnography: Principles in Practice*. (3rd Ed.). London and New York: Routledge.

Hallowell, A. I. (1955). The Ojibwa Self and Its Behavioral Environment. In Hallowell, *Culture and Experience*. Philadelphia: University of Pennsylvania Press.

Hatt, B. (2007). Street Smarts vs. Book Smarts: The Figured World of Smartness in the Lives of Marginalized, Urban Youth. *The Urban Review*, 39 (2 June 2007). DOI: 10.1007/s11256-007-0047-9.

Heath, S. B. (1983). *Ways with Words*. Cambridge: Cambridge University Press.

Heath, S.B. and Street, B.V. (2008). *On Ethnography: Approaches to Language and Literacy Research (An NCRLL Volume)*. New York and London: Teachers College Press.

Higgleton, E., Sargeant, H. and Seaton, A. (Eds.). (1997). *Chambers Pocket Dictionary*. Edinburgh: Chambers Harrap Publishers Ltd.

Hobart, M. (1993). Introduction: The Growth of Ignorance. In M. Hobart (Ed.). *An Anthropological Critique of Development: The Growth of Ignorance*. London: Routledge.

Hodges, D. C. (1998). Participation as Dis-Identification With/in a Community of Practice. *Mind, Culture and Identity*, 5, 4, 272–90.

Holland, D. and Cole, M. (1995). Between Discourse and Schema: Reformulating a Cultural-Historical Approach to Culture and Mind. *Anthropology & Education Quarterly*, 26, 4, 475–90.

Holland, D., Lachicotte Jr. W., Skinner, D. and Cain, C. (1998). *Identity and Agency in Cultural Worlds*. Cambridge: Harvard University Press.

Holliday, A. (1999). Small Cultures. *Applied Linguistics*, 20, 2, 237–64.

Hudelson, S. (1994). Literacy Development of Second Language Children. In F. Genesee (Ed.). *Educating Second Language Children: The Whole Child, the Whole Curriculum, the Whole Community*. Cambridge: Cambridge University Press.

Inden, R. (1990). *Imagining India*. Oxford: Blackwell.

Ivanic, R. (1997). *Writing and Identity*. Amsterdam: John Benjamins.

Jeke C. G. (2006). Malawi Situation Analysis of Evaluation Practices on Non-Formal Education (NFE) and Literacy Programmes: Reinforcing National Capacities to Evaluate Non-formal Education and Literacy Programmes for Young People and Adults. A Paper Presented at Cross-National Training Workshop on Evaluating NFE and Literacy Programmes for Youths and Adults (20–23 February 2006, Hamburg, Germany.

Jurow, A. S. (2005). Shifting Engagements in Figured Worlds: Middle School Mathematics Students' Participation in an Architectural Design Project. *The Journal of Learning Sciences*, 14, 1, 35–67. Downloaded from http://www.jstor.org/stable/1466882.

Kachiwanda, S. O. (2009). *Everyday Literacy Practices among Minority Language Speakers of Ciyawo in Malawi: Issues of Language Choice in Written Texts*. (PhD Thesis). Lancaster: Lancaster University.

Kadzamira, E. and Rose, P. (2003). Can Free Primary Education Meet the Needs of the Poor?: Evidence from Malawi. *International Journal of Educational Development*, 23, 501–16.

Kafakoma, R. and Mageza, Q. (2007). *End of Programme Evaluation of the Socio-Economic Empowerment Programme for Poverty Reduction: Final Report*. Lilongwe: Ministry of Women and Child Development.

Kalman, J. (2005a). Mothers to Daughters, *Pueblo to Ciudad*: Women's Identity Shifts in the Construction of a Literate Self. In A. Rogers (Ed.). *Urban*

Literacy: Communication, Identity and Learning in Development Contexts. Hamburg: UNESCO Institute for Education.

Kalman, J. (2005b). *Discovering Literacy: Access Routes to Written Culture for a Group of Women in Mexico*. Hamburg: UNESCO Institute for Education.

Kamtengeni, L. (1999). *Reasons for Participation in the NALP for Malawi and Ways in Which Literacy Skills are Utilized*. (Master's Thesis). University of Toronto: Toronto, Canada.

Kayambazinthu, E. (2003). Language Rights and the Role of Minority Languages in National Development in Malawi. *Current Issues in Language Planning*, 4, 2, 146–60.

Kell, C. (2009). Literacy Practices, Text/s and Meaning Making Across Time and Space. In M. Baynham and M. Prinsloo (Eds.). *The Future of Literacy Studies*. Hampshire: Palgrave Macmillan.

Kepe, T. (1999). The Problem of Defining Community: Challenges for the Lna Reform Programme in Rural South Africa. *Development Southern Africa*, 16, 3, 415–33. DOI: 10.0180/03768359908440089.

Kiely, R. (1999). *The Last Refuge of the Noble Savage? A Critical Assessment of Post-Development Theory*. Accessed on 4/5/11 from http://dx.doi.org/10.1080/09578819908426726.

Kingsbury, D. (2004). Introduction. In D. Kingsbury, J. Remenyi, J. MacKay and J. Hunt. (Eds.). *Key Issues in Development*. New York: Palgrave Macmillan.

Kishindo, P.J. (1994). The Impact of a National Language on Minority Languages: The Case of Malawi. *Journal of Contemporary African Studies*. 12, 2, 127–150.

Knight, P. T. (2002). *Small-Scale Research*. London: SAGE Publications Ltd.

Kress, G. (2010). *Multimodality: A Social Semiotic Approach to Contemporary Communication*. New York: Routledge.

Krueger, R. A. (1994). *Focus Group: A Practical Guide for Applied Research*. (2nd Ed.). Thousand Oaks: SAGE Publications Inc.

Kuthemba Mwale, J. B. (1990). *Malawi National Adult Education and Literacy Program: An Impact Evaluation*. CERT. Zomba Malawi.

Lamba, I. C. (1984). *The History of Post-war Western Education in Colonial Malawi 1945-61: A Study of the Formulation and Application of Policy*. (PhD Thesis). University of Edinburgh.

Latour, B. (2005). *Reassembling the Social: An Introduction to Actor-Network-Theory*. Oxford: Oxford University Press.

Lave, J. and Wenger, E. (1991). *Situated Learning: Legitimate Peripheral Participation*. Cambridge: Cambridge University Press.

Linda, G. (1982). Focus Groups: A New Look at an Old Friend. *Marketing and Media Decisions*, 17, 10, 96, 98.

Lukes, S. (2007). Power and the Battle for Hearts and Minds: On the Bluntness of Soft Power. In F. Berenskoetter and M. J. Williams (Eds.). *Power in World Politics*. London and New York: Routledge.

Lukes, S. (2005). Power: *A Radical Review*. (2nd Ed.). Hampshire: Palgrave Macmillan.

Luttrell, W. and Parker, C. (2001). High School Students' Literacy Practices and Identities, and the Figured World of School. *Journal of Research in Reading*, 24, 3, 235–47. Downloaded from http://eds.b.ebscohost.com/eds/pdfviewer/pdfviewer?vid=8&sid=55db3944-9c55-4d7a-8048-c045f540fce8%40sessionmgr110&hid=127

Madden, R. (2010). *Being Ethnographic: A Guide to the Theory and Practice of Ethnography*. Los Angeles: SAGE Publications Ltd.

Maddox, B. (2008). What Good Is Literacy? Insights and Implications of the Capabilities Approach. *Journal of Human Development*, 9, 2. DOI: 10.1080/14649880802078736.

Malawi Government (2000). *Interim Poverty Reduction and Growth Strategy Paper*. Lilongwe. Malawi Government.

Malawi Government (2002). *Malawi Poverty Reduction Strategy Paper: Final Draft*. Lilongwe: Malawi Government.

Malawi Government (2012). *Malawi Growth and Strategy II: 2011–2016*. Lilongwe: Ministry of Finance and Development Planning.

Martin-Jones, M. (2000). Enterprising women: multilingual literacies in the construction of new identities. In M. Martin-Jones and K. Jones (Eds.). *Multilingual Literacies: Reading and writing Different Worlds*. Amsterdam: John Benjamins Publishing Company.

Maruatona, T. and Cervero, R.M. (2004). Adult Literacy Education in Botswana: Planning between Reproduction and Resistance. *Studies in the Education of Adults*. 36, 2, 235–51. DOI:10.1080/02660830.2004.11661499.

McCaffery, J., Merrifield, J. and Millican, J. (2007). *Developing Adult Literacy: Approaches to Planning, Implementing, and Delivering Literacy Initiatives*. Oxford: Oxfam.

Miles, B. and Huberman, A. M. (1994). *Qualitative Data Analysis: An Expanded Sourcebook*. (2nd Ed.). Thousand Oaks: SAGE Publication.

Millican, J. (2004). 'I will stay here until I die': A Critical Analysis of the Muthande Literacy Programme. In A. Robinson-Pant (Ed.). *Women, Literacy and Development: Alternative Perspectives*. London and New York: Routledge.

Milner, G., Mulera, D., Chimuzu Banda, T., Mutale, E. and Chimombo, J. (2011). *Trends in Achievement Levels of Grade 6 Learners in Malawi*. SACMEQ Policy Brief No.1 www.sacmeq.org

Ministry of Economic Planning and Development (1995). *Policy Framework for Poverty Alleviation Programme*. MEPD: Lilongwe.

Ministry of Education (2007). *Education for All: The Malawi Language Policy in Education (Draft)*. Lilongwe: Ministry of Education.

Ministry of Education, Science and Technology (2008). *National Education Sector Plan 2008–2017: A Statement*. Lilongwe: MEST.

Ministry of Education Science and Technology (2013). *Education Statistics 2012*. Lilongwe: Ministry of Education Science and Technology.

Ministry of Gender, Child Welfare, and Community Services (2004). *A National Strategic Plan for the United Nations Literacy Decade 2003-2012 (Draft)*. Lilongwe: Malawi Government.

Ministry of Gender, Child Welfare, and Community Services (2005). *Adult Education and Literacy in Malawi: Issues, Challenges and the Way Forward*. A Paper Presented at the National Education Conference at Malawi Institute of Management 1 April 2005.

Ministry of Women and Children Affairs and Community Services (2005). *The National Adult Literacy Programme (NALP): A Strategy for Enhancing National Development Education*. Lilongwe: NCLAE.

Ministry of Women and Child Development (2008). *The Development and State of Adult Learning and Education (ALE): A National Report of Malawi*. Lilongwe: The Government of Malawi.

Mipando, C. and Higgs, P. (1982). *A Guide to the Curriculum for Literacy and Adult Education in Malawi*. Lilongwe: Department of Community Services.

Mjaya, A. N. U. (2010). *National Adult Literacy Programme and the Use of Minority Languages in Malawi: The Case of Ciyawo*. (Master's Thesis). Zomba: Chancellor College.

Mjaya, A. N. U. (2011). *Towards Understanding Malawi's National Adult Literacy Programme: A Discourse Analysis*. (Master's Thesis). Norwich: UEA.

Mosse, D. (2004). Is Good Policy Unimplementable? Reflections on the Ethnography of Aid Policy and Practice. *Development and Change*, 35, 4, 639-71.

Mosse, D. (2005). *Cultivating Development: An Ethnography of Aid Policy and Practice*. London: Pluto Press.

Mpheluka, G. (1983). *Functional Literacy Pilot Programmes in Malawi: A Report on the Review of the Functional Literacy Pilot Programmes*. Zomba: Centre for Social Research.

Mumisa, M. (2002). Islam and Proselytism in South Africa and Malawi. *Journal of Muslim Minority Affairs*, 22, 2, 175-298. DOI: 10.1080/136020002200027285.

Nabi, R., Rogers, A. and Street, B. (2009). *Hidden Literacies: Ethnographic Studies of Literacy and Numeracy Practices*. Bury St Edmunds: Uppingham Press.

Nasution, A. H. (1969). *From Traditional to Functional Literacy and Development*. Ibadan: Institute of African Adult Education, University of Ibadan.

National Statistical Office (2010). *Population and Housing Census: Education and Literacy*. Zomba: NSO.

Openjuru, G., Baker, D., Rogers, A. and Street, B. (2016) (Eds.). *Exploring Adult Literacy and Numeracy Practices: Ethnographic Case Studies from Uganda*. Bury St Edmunds: Uppingham Press.

OSISA (2007). *Adult Literacy: Putting Southern African Policy and Practice into Perspectives*. Downloaded on 16/06/11 from http://www.osisa.org/resources/docs/PDFs/AdultLiteracy.pdf.

Oxenham, J. (1980). *Literacy: Writing, Reading and Social Organisation*. London: Routledge and Kegan Paul.

Papen, U. (2002). *TVs, Textbooks and Tour Guides: Uses and Meanings of Literacy in Namibia*. (PhD Thesis). Kings College, Department of Education and Professional Studies.

Papen, U. (2004). Literacy and Development: What Works for Whom? Or How Relevant is the Social Practices View of Literacy for Literacy Education in Developing Countries? *International Journal of Educational Development*, 25 (2005), 5–17. DOI: 10.1016/j.ijedudev.2004.05.001.

Papen, U. (2005). *Adult Literacy as a Social Practice: More Than Skills*. London: Routledge

Pemagbi, J. and Rogers, A. (1996). *Literacy Enhancement in English in West Africa. Guidebook for the Production and Use of Real and Learner-Generated Materials*. Reading: Education for Development.

Phiri, M. A. R. and Safalaoh, A. C. L. (2003). *Evaluation of the National Adult Literacy Programme (First Draft)*. Lilongwe: The Department of Economic Planning and Development.

Plant, R. (1974). *Community and Ideology: An Essay in Applied Social Philosophy*. London: Routledge and Kegan Paul.

Prinsloo, M. and Breier, M. (Eds.). (1996). *The Social Uses of Literacy. Theory and Practice in Contemporary South Africa*. Bertsham, South Africa and Amsterdam: Sached Books and John Benjamins.

Quinn, N. and Holland, D. (1987). Culture and Cognition. In D. Holland and N. Quinn (Eds.). *Cultural Models in Language and Thought*. Cambridge: Cambridge University Press.

Robinson, C. (2007). Figured World of History Learning in a Social Studies Methods Classroom. *The Urban Review*, 39, 2, June 2007. DOI: 10.1007/s11256-007-0046-x.

Robinson, C. (2014). *Languages in Adult Literacy: Policies and Practices during the 15 Years of EFA (2000–2015). Paper commissioned for the EFA Global Monitoring Report 2015, Education for All 2000–2015: achievements and challenges*. Paris: UNESCO.

Robinson-Pant, A. (2001a). Women's Literacy and Health: Can an Ethnographer Find the Links? In B. Street (Ed.). *Literacy and Development: Ethnographic Perspectives*. London: Routledge.

Robinson-Pant, A. (2001b). Development as a Discourse: What Relevance to Education? In *Compare*, 31, 3. DOI: 10.1080/3057920120098464.

Robinson-Pant, A. (2001). *Why Eat Green Cucumber at the Time of Dying? Exploring the Link Between Women's Literacy and Development: A Nepal Perspective*. Hamburg: UNESCO Institute for Education.

Robinson-Pant, A. (2008). 'Why Literacy Matters': Exploring a Policy Perspective on Literacies, Identities and Social Change. *Journal of Development Studies*, 44, 6, 779–96.

Robinson-Pant, A. and Singal, N. (2013). Researching Ethically across Cultures: Issues of Knowledge, Power and Voice. *Compare: A journal of Comparative and International Education (Special Issue)*, 43, 4, 417–21.

Rogers, A. (1994). *Using Literacy: A New Approach to Post-Literacy Materials*. London: Overseas Development Administration, Serial No. 10.

Rogers, A. (1999). Improving the Quality of Adult Literacy Programmes in Developing Societies: The 'Real Literacies' Approach. *International Journal of Educational Development*, 19, 219–34.

Rogers, A. (2004). *Non-formal Education: Flexible Schooling or Participatory Education*. Hong Kong: Hong Kong University Press.

Rogers, A. (2008). *The ICEIDA-Supported REFLECT Programme in Monkey Bay, Malawi: A Progress Review*. ICEIDA.

Rogers, A. (2008). Comparative Study of the Malawi-REFLECT Programme and the Uganda -FAL Programme and Suggestions for Future Strategies. ICEIDA Report.

Rogers, A. (2014). *The Base of the Iceberg: Informal Learning and Its Impact on Formal and Non-formal Learning*. Opladen: Barbara Budrich Publishers.

Rogers, A., Kachiwanda, S. and McKay, V. (2003). *Literacy, Communication and Development*. Report of a Consultancy Undertaken for DFID-Malawi, March–April 2003.

Rogers, A., Maddox, B., Millican, J., Newell Jones, K., Papen, U. and Robinson-Pant, A. (1999). *Re-defining Post-literacy in a Changing World*. London: Department for International Development, Education Research, Serial No. 29.

Rogers, A. and Street, B. (2009). An Ethnographic Approach to Literacy and Numeracy in Pakistan. In R. Nabi, A. Rogers and B. Street (Eds.). *Hidden Literacies: Ethnographic Studies of Literacy and Numeracy Practices*. Bury St Edmunds: Uppingham Press.

Rokadiya, B. C. (1986). *National Adult Literacy Programme: An Outline of the Curriculum*. Lilongwe: NCLAE.

Rubin, B. C. (2007). Learner Identity Amid Figured Worlds: Constructing (In)competence at an Urban High School. *The Urban Review*, 39, 2. DOI: 10.1007/s11256-007-0044-z.

Rush, L. S., Fecho, B. (2008). When Figured Worlds Collide: Improvisation in an Inquiry Classroom. *Teaching Education*, 19, 2, 123–36. DOI: 10.1080/10476210802040781.

Ryan, J.W. (1985). Language and Literacy: The Planning of Literacy Activities in Multilingual States. In G. Carron and A. Bordia (Eds.). *Issues in Planning and Implementing National Literacy Programmes*. Paris: UNESCO.

Sanjek, R. (1990). *Fieldnotes: The Making of Anthropology*. Ithaca and London: Cornell University Press.

SARN (2010). *What is REFLECT?* Accessed on 26/12/2014 from http://www.sareflect.org/index.php?option=com_content&view=category&id=38&layout=blog&Itemid=55.

Scriber, S. and Cole, M. (1981). *The Psychology of Literacy*. Massachusetts: Harvard University Press.

Selznick, P. (1992). *The Moral Commonwealth: Social Theory and the Promise of Community*. Berkley and Los Angeles: University of California Press.

Selznick, P. (1996). In Search of Community. In K. Vitek and W. Jackson (Eds.). *Rooted in the Land: Essays on Community and Place*. New Haven: Yale University Press.

Shamim, F. and Qureshi, R. (2013). Informed Consent in Educational Research in the South: Tensions and Accommodations. *Compare: A journal of Comparative and International Education (Special Issue)*, 43, 4, 464–82.

Shweder, R. A. (1991). *Thinking through Cultures: Expeditions in Cultural Psychology*. Cambridge, MA: Harvard University Press.

Skutnabb-Kangas, T. and McCarty, T.L. (2006). Key Concepts in Bilingual Education: Ideological, Historical, Epistemological, and Empirical Foundations. In J. Cummins and N. Hornberger (Eds.). *Bilingual Education, vol. 5 Encyclopedia (sic) of Language and Education*, (2nd Ed.). New York: Springer.

St. Clair, R. (2010). *Why Literacy Matters: Understanding the Effects of Literacy Education for Adults*. Leicester: niace.

Storey, A. (2009). Measuring Human Development. In G. McCann, and S. McCloskey (Eds.). *From the Local to the Global: Key Issues in Development* Studies. (2nd Ed.). London: Pluto Press.

Street, B.V. (2009). New Literacies in Theory and Practice: What Are the Implications for Language in Education? *Linguistics and Education*, 10, 1, 1–24.

Street, B. V. (1984). *Literacy in Theory and Practice*. Cambridge: Cambridge University Press.

Street, B. V. (1993). Introduction: The New Literacy Studies. In B. V. Street (Ed.). *Cross-cultural Approaches to Literacy*. Cambridge: Cambridge University Press.

Street, B. V. (2000). Literacy Events and Literacy Practices: Theory and Practice in the New Literacy Studies. In M. Martin-Jones and K. Jones (Eds.). *Multilingual Literacies*. Amsterdam/Philadelphia: John Benjamin Publishing Company.

Street, B. V. (2001). Introduction. In B.V. Street (Ed.). *Literacy and Development: Ethnographic Perspectives*. London and New York: Routledge.

Street, B. V. (2003). What's 'new' in New Literacy Studies? Critical Approaches to Literacy in Theory and Practice. *Current Issues in Comparative Education*, 5, 2.

Street, B. V. (2009). The Future of 'Social Literacies.' In M. Baynham and M. Prinsloo (Eds.). *The Future of Literacy Studies*. Hampshire: Palgrave Macmillan.

Street, B. V. (2010). Literacy Inequalities in Theory and Practice: The Power to Name and Define. *International Journal of Educational Development*, 31 (2011), 580–6

Street, B.V. and Lefstein, A. (2007). *Literacy: An Advanced Resource Book*. New York: Routledge.

The Government of the Republic of Malawi (2007). *The National Adult Literacy Policy: Final Draft*. Lilongwe: Ministry of Women and Child Development.

Thompson, S. (2015). Literacy Mediation in Neighbourhood Houses. *Australian Journal of Adult Learning*, 55, Number 3, November 2015.

Townley, B. (1993). Foucault, Power/ Knowledge, and Its Relevance for Human Resource Management. *Academy of Management Review*, 18, 3, 518–45.

UNDP (1990). *Human Development Report 1990*. New York: Oxford University Press.

UNESCO (2000). *The Dakar Framework of Action*. Paris: UNESCO.

UNESCO (2004). *The Plurality of Literacy and Its Implications for Policies and Programmes: Position Paper*. Paris: UNESCO.

UNESCO (2005). *Education For All Global Monitoring Report: Literacy for Life 2006*. Paris: UNESCO.

Urrieta Jr. L. (2007). Figured Worlds and Education: An Introduction to the Special Issue. *The Urban Review*, 39, 2. DOI: 10.1007/s11256-007-0051-0.

Vale, I. and Weiss, E. (2009). Participation in a Figured World of Graffiti. *Teaching and Teacher Education* 26 (2010), 128–35.

Vail, L. and White, L. (1989). Tribalism in the Political History of Malawi. In L. Vail (Ed.). *The Creation of Tribalism in Southern Africa*. London: James Currey.

Wagner, D. A. (1992). Literacy: Developing the Future. *International Yearbook of Education Volume XLIII*. Paris: UNESCO.

Wagner, D. A. (1993). *Literacy, Culture and Development: Becoming Literate in Morocco*. Cambridge: Cambridge University Press.

Wardhaugh, R. (1990). *An Introduction to Sociolinguistics*. Oxford: Basil Blackwell.

WCEFA Inter-Agency Commission (1990). *Meeting Basic Learning Needs: A Vision for the 1990s*. New York: Inter-Agency Commission.

Wenger, E. (1998). *Communities of Practice: Learning, Meaning, and Identity*. Cambridge: Cambridge University Press.

Wenger, E., McDermott, R. and Snyder, W. M. (2002). *A Guide to Managing Knowledge: Cultivating Communities of Practice*. Massachusetts: Harvard Business School Press.

Wenger, E. and Wenger-Trayner, B. (2015). *Communities of Practice: A Brief Introduction* – V 15 April 2015. Accessed on 24/12/2016 from http://wenger-trayner.com/introduction-to-communities-of-practice/

Willis, K. (2005). *Theories and Practices of Development*. London and New York: Routledge.

World Food Programme (2016). *Malawi: Current Issues and What the World Food Programme is Doing*. https://www.wfp.org/countries/Malawi.

Index

absentees 95
adult learners 46–9, 73, 81, 113, 127
adult literacy 3–4
   learners (*See* literacy learners)
   learning 18–19, 24, 81
   in Malawi 112–15
adult literacy class 1–12, 18, 35, 39–41, 43, 48, 91–107
   bureaucracy in non-formal settings 92–6
   discipline measures 96–7, 99
   punctuality 99
   school and expectations 100–3
   songs in, singing 98–100
   special lessons 98–100
   suspension of literacy lessons in 25, 92–5
   teacher-centred approach 97
agricultural leaflet 56–8
Anderson, B. 26
artefacts 16, 20–1, 35–6, 47, 53
   and figured worlds 24
   FISP coupons 59
   pens and inkpads 24, 67–9
   Social Cash Transfer Programme leaflet 61–2
authorship 23
autonomous model of literacy 4, 14

Barton, D. 15–16, 20, 27
behavioural environments 17
Blot, R. K. 17

Chichewa 3, 5
   lesson 32, 40–1, 86
   literacy 40, 48, 86, 103–5, 109, 128
   in Malawi Social Cash Transfer Programme Leaflet 61
   resident instructor 86–7
Ciyawo 5, 38, 111, 117–19, 122, 123
Cole, M. 142
Collins, J. 17

communities 12, 18, 26–7, 44
   savings group 33
Community Development Scheme 5–6
community member 1–2, 13, 15–17, 20, 23–4, 29–32, 37, 39–45, 47, 96
   literacy practices (*See* literacy practices)
   money card 62–4
   ration card 54–6
Community Social Support Committee (CSSC) 61, 64
cultural means 19–20
culture 18–19, 27–8, 35–6

Davies, B. 23, 71, 125, 142
decision-making process 25, 91, 95, 103, 107, 130
Delanty, G. 27
discourse 7–9, 11, 16, 23
   models 19–20
discursive positionality 22–3
District Community Development Officer 94
domain 20–1
Draft National Adult Literacy Policy 9, 113, 116

educated learners 71–7, 84, 88
emergency food assistance programme 54–6
English literacy 23, 33, 40–1, 74, 104–6, 109, 119, 127, 128, 143
Escobar, A. 11
ethnographer 47
   as benefactor 49–50
   as co-instructor 48
   as resource person 47–8
ethnographic approach 5, 47, 50, 144, 146

farming 56–9
Farm Input Subsidy Programme (FISP) 59
FGD. *See* focus group discussions (FGD)

figurative identity 26
figured worlds 2–3, 5, 13, 17–20, 29, 35–6, 53–4
   of adult literacy learning 18–19, 24
   agency in 21–2, 128–31
   artefacts and 24, 138–42
   authoring and re-authoring identities 135–8
   conceptualization of 17–18
   and domain 20–1
   of emergency food assistance programme 54–6
   improvisation in 22, 128–31
   issues 18
   of modern farming 56–9
   objectification in 21
   and power 19
   resistance in 128–31
   of Social Cash Transfer Programme 59–64
   socially and culturally 18
   ultra-poor and labour constrained 60–1, 64
focus group discussions (FGD) 35
food assistance programme 54–6
food-insecurity 54, 56
formal literacy learning 95–6
functional knowledge 18

Gee, J. P. 19
Gereluk, D. 27
Government of the Republic of Malawi, The 113

Hallowell, A. I. 17
Hamilton, M. 15, 20, 27
Harré, R. 23, 71, 125, 142
Holland, D. 142
   artefact 16, 24, 35–6
   authorship 23
   figured worlds 2–3, 5, 13, 17–22, 29, 35–6
   human agency 22
   identity, conceptualization of 25–6
   positionality 22–3
   theory of self and identity 2, 13, 17–18, 22, 25, 35
Holliday, A. 27
human agency 22, 91, 128

identity 1, 5, 27
   artefacts and 138–42
   authoring and re-authoring 135–8
   conceptualization of 25–6
   figurative 26
   in NLS 16–17
   positional/relational 26
   in reading and writing 71–90
   theory of 2, 13, 17–18, 22, 25, 35
illiteracy 5–6, 8–11, 18–19, 68, 87
improvisation 22
Inden, R. 22
informal interviews 34–5
informed consent 46–7
ink pads 24, 67–9
instructors 86–9
   power and suspension of literacy lessons 92–5
intelligent learners 81–5, 88–9
intentional worlds 17
interactive positioning 23, 71, 78, 82, 84, 87

Kachiwanda, S. O. 46
knowledgeable/not knowledgeable learners 77–81, 89
Knowles, M. S. 92, 100
kulemba ndi kuwerenga 5

language(s) 109–10, 123–4
   defining 112
   formal and informal 114–16
   in Malawi 62, 111–14
   multilingualism 110–11, 144
   teaching literacy 116–23
learners. *See* literacy learners
literacy 11–12, 16
   class (*See* adult literacy class)
   development 6–11
   events 14–16
   ideological model 14, 17
   instrumental views of 11
   mediation 16, 64–7
   officers 91
   policy perspectives 8–12
   rates 3
   as social practice 4, 18, 26, 29
   social theory of 13–16
   theory 142–3

literacy learners
  Chichewa 104
  educated and uneducated 71–7
  gifted 84
  instructors and 86–9, 92, 97
  knowledgeable and not knowledgeable 77–81
  primary schooling 84
  struggling and intelligent 81–5
  suspension of literacy lessons 92–5
literacy learning and positioning 131–4
literacy practices 2, 5, 13–18, 20–1, 25, 53
  classroom 84, 87
  emergency food assistance programme 54–6
  FISP 59
  modern farming 56–9
  Social Cash Transfer Programme 59–64
literacy research 3–5
  artefacts in 36
  community member, becoming 29–31
  dilemmas and opportunities 41–5
  ethical dilemmas 46–7
  ethnographer 47–50
  methodology 144–6
  methods 31–6
  site, locating 36–7
Lukes, S. 24–5, 91

McCarty, T. L. 110
Malawi 3
  adult literacy in 112–14
  food-insecurity in 54, 56
  literacy research in 3–5
  national language policy in 111–12
  traditional leaders, hierarchies of 38
Malawi Congress Party (MCP) 111–12
Malawi Government 3, 4, 6, 8–11, 49, 54, 56, 58, 125, 131, 141
Malawi Growth and Development Strategy II 10
Malawi National Functional Adult Literacy Programme 6
Malawi Poverty Reduction Strategy (MPRS) 8–9
Mang'anjas 38

Martin-Jones, M. 111
mediation 16, 64–7
Millican, J. 126
Ministry of Education 112
Ministry of Education Science and Technology 9
Ministry of Women and Children Affairs and Community Services 56
modern farming 56–9
modernity 9, 11
money card 62–4
Mponela Mass Education Pilot Project 5, 9
MPRS. *See* Malawi Poverty Reduction Strategy (MPRS)
Mtukula Pakhomo 59
multilingualism 110–11, 144

Nasution, A. H. 8
National Adult Literacy Programme (NALP) 1–2, 4–10, 48, 56, 112, 115, 116, 124, 126, 131, 134, 143
  history of 5–6
  levels in 7
  objectives 6, 56
  traditional leaders and 38
national language policy 111–12
National Literacy Committee 6
New Literacy Studies (NLS) 2, 5, 14, 16
  power and identity in 16–17
non-formal literacy learning 92–6
non-literate 3, 6–10, 16, 64, 68
Nyanja language 111

objectification 21
odziwa kulemba ndi kuwerenga 5
one-size-fits-all approach 53, 114, 124
osadziwa kulemba ndi kwerenga 5

Papen, U. 14–17
participant observation 31–3
peer learning 89
Pemagbi, J. 123
pens 24, 67–9
Phiri, M. A. R. 114
pilot functional literacy project 6
Plant, R. 27
policy perspectives 8–12

positional identity 26
positioning 22–3, 71–2, 74, 80, 125, 134, 139, 142
poverty 8–9, 60
power 4, 91
  conceptualization of 24–5
  in literacy learning 125–8
  in NLS 16–17
  in reading and writing 71–90
  struggles for 91–107
Protracted Relief and Recovery Operation (PRRO) 54

Quinn, N. 17
Qureshi, R. 46

ration card 54–6
reflexive positioning 23, 71, 78, 82–4, 89
relational identity 26
research. *See* literacy research
Robinson-Pant, A. 144
Rogers, A. 123
Rokadiya, B. C. 6–7, 115

Safalaoh, A. C. L. 114
Sawabu 13, 16, 25, 36–7
  allegiances 43–4
  cultural complications 30–1
  historical perspectives of 37–8
  literacy centre 111
  literacy classroom in 39–41
  literacy officers 91
  Malekano trading centre 41–2
  people of 38–9
  schools in 42–4
  security in 30
  social activities 44
  traditional leadership in 38
  Tupoce clinic 45
  video showroom at Malekano 44
  water sources 45
  Weca family, houses cluster for 37
school culture 32, 91, 96–8, 126, 137
self, theory of 2, 13, 17–18, 22, 25, 35
semi-structured interviews 34
Shamim, F. 46

Shweder, R. A. 17
simplified worlds 17
Skutnabb-Kangas, T. 110
Social Cash Transfer Programme 59, 138
  aim of 59–60
  beneficiary identification process 61
  CSSC, execution with 61
  figured world of 60
  leaflet 61–2
  registration slip 60–1
  ultra-poor and labour constrained 60–1, 64
social change 12, 18, 131–4
social communities 18
social practice 4, 13–14, 16, 18, 25–6, 29
social theory of literacy 2, 13–17, 19–20, 53, 67
special lessons 98–100
St. Clair, R. 17
Street, B. V. 4, 14–15, 17, 27
struggling learners 81–5
sukulu za kwacha 7
supervisor 86
  cluster 29–31, 34, 39, 41, 91
  and instructor 95
  positioning 74, 80, 82, 137
suspension of literacy lessons 25, 92–5
systematic literacy 4

teaching literacy 116–23
thumb printing 59, 68–9
traditional knowledge 10

Ukani Traditional Literacy Programme 7
uneducated learners 71–7, 84

Wenger, E. 25
Willis, K. 11
World Conference on Education for All (WCEFA) 11
World Food Programme (WFP) 54

Yawos 38–9

zogwa manyumba 54

www.ingramcontent.com/pod-product-compliance
Lightning Source LLC
Chambersburg PA
CBHW061838300426
44115CB00013B/2431